Reviews by Experienc__ ıanners

"Get this book. You'll be amazed at the unexpected ease of the process and more importantly your results." – *Jim Riggs, author, Blue Mountain Buckskin. Tanner of hundreds of hides, teacher of hundreds of tanners.*

"Using fresh hides and the Deerskins into Buckskins method has made tanning so much easier. I'm addicted." – *Molly Miller, professional brain tanner for 12 years.*

"Deerskins into Buckskins has turned me into a wetscraper...its just plain easier. Can you believe it?!" – *David Rose, professional brain tanner, a dry scraper for 20 years, and director of the River Spirit School of Natural Living.*

"The best tanning book I've ever seen. Matt got everything right." – *Jack McKey, brain tanner for 45 years who has spent uncountable time tanning with Native Americans from Florida to Alaska*

"I learned something on the very first page I looked at." – *Tom Orr, professional brain tanner for 30 years.*

"This method definitely makes it easier for our students." – *Tamarack Song, director of the Teaching Drum Outdoor School.*

"Deerskins into buckskin will alow the reader to trade the time it takes to read this book for MANY YEARS of trial and eror. I have over 40 years exprience tannen hides if I would of only had this book back then." – *Loyd Arthur, North Eastern, OK.*

"I would not recommend learning to tan without this book...unless you have an expert living with you!" – *Patrick Farneman, St. George, UT.*

Reviews by Magazines

"By far the best book on the subject!" – *Carla Emery, author, The Encyclopedia of Country Living.*

"Matt Richards brings tanning to a level of simplicity that is accessible to anyone. Experimentation combined with years of tanning for a living and a thorough study of leather chemistry, has resulted in a simple method that produces excellent results." – *American Survival Guide.*

"Proves to be a comprehensive guide to natural leather making." – *American Library Association, BOOKLIST.*

"Information and practical advice you won't find in any other book. Easy to read yet amazingly thorough, with just a touch of twisted humor in the right places. A terrific resource!" – *Susan Jennys, Muzzleblasts.*

"The author's intimate understanding of deerskins, tools, processes, and problems bears witness to a tremendous depth of knowledge about his craft. Deerskins into Buckskins is a highly recommendable work....this book deserves a place on your bookshelf." – *Scott Jones, Bulletin of Primitive Technology.*

"At a time when outdoor wear is dominated by plastic wonder fabrics it is refreshing to see a book on how to make a comfortable and warm material from a natural resource that would otherwise be cast aside. Deerskins into Buckskins teaches this art with wit, clarity and ease." – *Backwoodsman Magazine.*

"...contains the important details to brain tan in the simplest way known, cutting tanning time and effort in half." – *Blackpowder Hunter.*

"Easy to understand and useful if you're interested in preserving and using your deer hide to make a pair of trousers or leather gloves. Get started, buy a copy. Enjoy." – *Cody Beers, Wyoming Wildlife.*

Reviews by Novice Tanners

"If a guy couldn't tan a hide with this he should stay out of the woods!" – *Ted Fry, Raptor Archery.*

"Where other instruction books leave you saying, "Huh?", this one caters to those of us who REALLY have never done this before!" – *Carmiehead, KY.*

"My first hide turned out spectacularly, simply by following the instructions in the book. Even if you aren't into tanning hides, this book is just fun to read. It has humor and history and everything a great book should have!" – *Terri Cressman, Bethlehem, PA.*

"This book has many virtues, but the one I was most grateful for is that Matt made it impossible NOT to understand how to braintan. He anticipates the reader's every possible wrong turn. So many skilled craftsmen are tongue-tied. Even if they know what they are doing, they cannot put themselves into the mind of a newcomer to their craft. Matt not only has a rare knack for doing just that, he also knows how to keep the nervous newbie calm. Anyone who follows Matt's directions will have a beautiful piece of buckskin, soft as velvet but tough enough to turn the meanest thorns..." – *George Lee, Norfolk, VA.*

"After following Matt's method I ended up with soft buck skin the very first time with significantly less effort. Matt's book covers the subject in very good detail, covering the bucking/wetscrape tanning method, theory of how brain tanning works, the tools necessary including primitive tools, and the basics on how to make garnments. I think that if you are going to try brain tanning deerskin, this book is a must-have." – *Jonathan Jeffer, El Cerrito, CA.*

"I have successfully completed dozens of buckskins under the mentoring of numerous experts. It is obvious that Matt has created a 'quantum leap' in the art. His process dramatically reduces the time and work, resulting in the nicest buckskin I have ever made." – *Jeff 'Roadkill' Damm, engineer and backyard tanner.*

Deerskins into Buckskins

How to Tan With Brains, Soap or Eggs

by Matt Richards

2nd Edition
Revised & Updated

Backcountry Publishing
Cave Junction, Oregon

Published by:
Backcountry Publishing
1700 East Nevada St
Ashland OR 97520
www.braintan.com

Printed on recycled paper in the United States of America. Cover design and illustration by Lightbourne Images, copyright 1997.

2nd Edition: Revised & Updated

Library of Congress Cataloging-in-Publication Data

Richards, Matt
    Deerskins into buckskins: how to tan with brains, eggs or soap; 2nd edition, revised and updated / Matt Richards.
    240 p. ; 22 cm.
    LCCN: 97093709 (first edition)
    ISBN: 0965867242

    1. Buckskin. 2. Tanning. 3. Leather work. I. Title.

TS980.B82R52 2004   675.23

Quantity Purchases:
We offer substantial discounts on bulk sales to organizations, schools, and businesses. For more information write: backcountry@braintan.com

Contents

What's New

I've been tanning and teaching tanning for 15 years. Every once in awhile, one of my hides or one someone else was showing me, was insanely soft. Brain tanned buckskin is known for being lusciously soft, but the occasional hide was just completely, insanely soft. I've always wanted to know why.

A couple of years after *Deerskins into Buckskins* was first published, my wife, Michelle, and I took a trip from our home in NW Montana to an event in Idaho to teach tanning. I had a hide soaking in a bucket of brains that I hadn't gotten a chance to soften. So I threw it in the back of our pickup (Michelle wasn't willing to hold it on her lap), and we sped off. Two days later I took it out of the brains to wring it out and soften it in my spare time sitting around camp. By the time I softened that hide, the brains were quite sour, but that hide was incredible. Out of the thousand I had tanned, only a couple had ever been as soft as that one. I passed it around and everyone ooohed and aaahed. And the inevitable question in my mind, and others, was, why? Why was this one hide so damn soft?

A few years later, I had a batch of hides that I wanted to soften that day but the alkalinity hadn't rinsed out of them quickly, so I dumped them in some warm vinegar water to speed up the process. They lost all their alkalinity and started to swell a little on the acid side, but I was set to soften and just said 'screw it'. Those four hides were extremely easy to soften, and came out oh so soft. A tanning friend of mine was working with me and he was going 'this is great, this is just great!'. So the next round we 'acidified' half the hides, and didn't acidify the other half, and the difference was super clear.

I spent the better part of the next year trying to pin down exactly what was the best amount of acidity to introduce into the hide, (not that much), how to get the most predictable results, and how it could be done with traditional materials. I got a lot of feedback from our online forum, *The Hide Out!*, (www.braintan.com/hide-out), and learned about ammonium sulphate from Bob Kurasawe, which does much the same thing as vinegar but has some advantages. The result is short and sweet (see *Acidifying* page 90-92). For about 15 minutes additional work you get:

* Easier to soften hides
* Hides that come out super soft
* Hides that take the dressing even when dry, which in turn:
  → removes the variability of trying to get the 'perfect moisture content' before dressing
  → makes it much easier to get complete brain penetration on thick hides, which makes tanning thicker hides such as moose, elk or even thick deer, way less work.
  → Makes it so you can skip one of the wringing steps (which takes 15 minutes itself).

This step is such a great improvement that it is what really motivated me to put out this new edition. Other key new highlights include:

* Different skinning cuts for a better hide shape, p. 40-41.
* How to tan Moose, Elk & Antelope, p. 158-162.
* Bibliography (thorough and user-friendly), p. 223-231
* Important improvements to the *Bucking* process.
* Important improvements to the *Dressing* step-by-step, to ensure success for first-timers.
* A step-by-step guide to varying this books' *Basic Method* if you want to try the 'pre-smoking' method, or if you want to tan without the bucking step . See pages 136-139.

Acknowledgments

For the 2nd Edition

One of the great things about publishing a book on a skill such as tanning is all of the feedback you get. I shared the very best of my tanning knowledge with the world and then had thousands of people run with it from there. I got emails, letters and phone calls from tanners both expert and novice telling me their experiences and experiments. My wife, Michelle, deserves many thanks for all the work and energy she put into getting the first edition out there into the world.

Tanners

We created an ongoing on-line forum called *The Hide Out!* (www.braintan.com/hideout) where tanners ask and answer questions. When I started having success with the 'acidifying' step, I posted my process there, and asked some of the experienced tanners to try it out and tell me their results. This showed very quickly how to describe the process so that others could successfully follow it. Those folks also started experimenting with the different parameters and made it that much faster to pin down exactly what works and the easiest way to get there. Thanks to all of you (I won't name names or else I'll forget someone!). I would, however, like to particularly thank *Bob Kurasawe*. He is an experimenter much like myself, and has shared his frequent insights freely. I particularly thank him for telling me about Ammonium Sulphate and his experiences with it.

Billy Metcalf wrote an article for Braintan.com on how to make skinning cuts so that you end up with a fuller, more useable hide shape. After publication of the first edition I had several people tell me how to do this, but Billy really made it crystal clear. The new skinning cut information in this book is based on what Billy taught.

Then there are the many folks who brain tan for a living, who as a rule, have always shared their knowledge openly and freely, which is not that common with traditional arts such as this. Whenever I could, I've visited these folks and showed them exactly how I do it, in exchange for them showing me exactly how they do it. I'd like to particularly thank *Jim Riggs, David Rose, Steven Edholm, Tamara Wilder, Melvin Beattie, George Whitehouse, Sunny, Doug Crist, Molly Miller, Matt McMahan, Dave Bethke, Stephano Baldesci, Wes Housler, Tom Oar, Joe & Vicki Dinsmore, Darry Wood, The Maness's* and the many others who have openly shared their skills while we were tanning, hanging out around the camp fire, or online via *The Hide Out!*

Book Production Helpers

Thanks to Linda Serrano for her work on photos and various layout tasks and to Laurie Morton for illustrations and proofing.

Preparing to Tan

Why Buckskin?

The reasons why many people are learning to make buckskin are diverse:

You can fully utilize the products of your hunt, to make clothing that is ideal to hunt in. The smoky smell of buckskin will cover your human odors. It is quiet. Fringe will break up your form. Nothing goes through brush, thickets and all around hunting abuse as well as buckskin. For these reasons it has a long and strong tradition with America's hunters.

> "For this kind of hunting, no dress is so good as a buckskin suit and moccasins. The moccasins enable one to tread softly and noiselessly, while the buckskin suit is of a most inconspicuous color, and makes less rustling than any other material when passing among projecting twigs."
> *Teddy Roosevelt, "Hunting Trips of a Ranchman" 1885*

It is practical *and* beautiful: It makes great clothing, bags and many other useful items.

Deerskins go to waste by the hundreds of thousands in North America. There are around six million deer shot annually in the U.S. Of these only a fraction ever make it to a tannery, and there they are submitted to the chemical tanning process. While there is nothing inherently wrong with hunters leaving hides in the forest for the maggots and coyotes, why not use it in between?

It is available locally. Deer are hunted, and roadkills happen in every part of North America, from sea to shining sea, from farm-land to the suburbs.

You don't need to hunt or even support hunting. Deer are getting hunted and roadkills are happening throughout the country. Skins are going to rot or get used. I know vegetarians who make buckskin, because they value the natural recycling aspect of it.

It is natural. Buckskin was made by early humans all over the world with wood, bone and stone tools. If for some reason it was time to dispose of your buckskin, it will return naturally into the earth from which it came.

You can make it at home. All the tools and materials can be found around your own home. Find a log, a metal bar, some wood ashes, a bucket, rotten wood, and you are ready to go. Buckskin has always been a cottage industry. I've been making and selling buck-skin for my livelihood for twelve years. What I love about it is that I can do it anywhere. I can scrape hides on the bluff overlooking the river. Watch the eagles and osprey swooping about, the deer going to drink, and then jump-in whenever I get too hot...not a bad way to work.

You can make it in the wilderness. A basic skill to know for survival in the wilds.

It is easy to sew. It doesn't unravel, so you can lace it together with nice big stitches. And those stitches are easily made through soft porous buckskin.

What Is Buckskin?

Buckskin is a soft porous material that is made from animal skin with the aid of lubricants, physical manipulation and woodsmoke (usually). It can be made from any of the hoofed animals including deer, elk, antelope, sheep, goat, buffalo, even cow. It is the way that a skin is tanned that makes it buckskin, not the fact that it is made from a deer hide. The type of treatment buckskin receives leaves it in a state somewhere between a fabric and a leather, with some qualities all to its own. It is strong, durable, soft, washable and warm. It cuts the wind, allows your skin to breath and stretches with the movement of your body. It is definitely not waterproof. Buckskin is particularly valued as a durable yet comfortable outdoor clothing, though it is also excellent for pouches, moccasins and many other items.

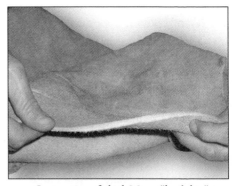

Cross section of thick Moose "buckskin"

Most leathers are soaked in chemicals that combine with the fibers and change them into an entirely new substance: leather. In the old days these chemicals were tannic acids derived from tree barks. Bark-tanned leathers were used for shoes, saddles and other items for which solidity or water repellency were valuable. They are still made by a few tanneries but most hides are currently tanned with chromic acids.

Chromic acids are very cheap to use but are unfortunately quite toxic. Pollution of waterways is the number one problem facing the modern leather tannery (as well as the folks downstream), and chrome compounds are the culprit. Most chrome tanneries have moved from the US and Europe, to countries where environmental laws are lax, such as India. Chrome-tanned leather is fairly soft and very stable when exposed to heat and rot. Its not as strong as buckskin and is broken down by the alkalinity of perspiration and soaps.

Chrome-tanned sheep and deer skins are currently marketed as "buckskin" even though they have very different physical properties than the traditional material. Traditional methods have not been industrialized because the tanning process relies on physical manipulation more than chemicals. This leaves it in the domain of the backyard tanner, where it has long been. The mystique and reputation of buckskin remains strong however and commercial interests will continue to cash in on it.

I like the old separation of leather and buckskin to refer to different categories of skin based fabrics. I'll use them this way throughout the book. You can use these terms however you want since everyone else does.

A Bit of History

When most people think of buckskin they envision long-fringed Indians on horseback or adventurous frontiersmen on a remote mountain hunt. Little do they know that it was once as common as blue jeans. Did you know that it was the work clothes of the common laborer in 18th century America and Europe? That General George Washington ordered buckskins to be made for the troops? Or that it was fashionable among the elite of Europe? Remember those images of men in powder white wigs, breeches and long stockings. Guess what those breeches were made of... Have you ever told a friend, "uh, that cost me a couple of bucks". Well that's because buckskin was such a common commodity of exchange in the American colonies that after the Revolution, buck became the slang for a dollar bill. But deer me, that's getting ahead of things, lets go back to the beginning.

Genesis iii 21: "Unto Adam also and to his wife did the Lord God make coats of skins, and clothed them."

The Stone Age

Stone age peoples, cavemen, and hunter gatherers all over the world had some things in common. Soaking hides in brains and pulling them soft seems to be one of them. It was part of the daily life of primitive peoples on every continent. There are accounts of brain and/or smoke tanning by the Zulus of southern Africa (brains), the Chukchee of eastern Russia (liver, urine and smoke), nomadic peoples of Asia (fermented milk, butter, and egg yolk), northern Asia (brains, liver and sour milk,) China (smoke), South America (smoke) and

Zulu Tanners in South Africa

North America (brains, smoke, liver, sweet corn, eggs, pine nuts, yucca root and a whole lot of other things!). Here's an account from Japan:

> "An oil tanning process which appears to be ancient, but which is still carried on in Japan.....
> To prepare Koshuinden leather, one starts with dried deerskin which has been soaked to the extent that the grain layer, together with the hair can be shaved away with a skiving knife. Tanning is accomplished by coating with animal brain matter or spinal-cord substance, for which mechanical tumbling, kneading, and staking probably are indispensable. A smoke tanning now follows, according the description of Sawayama..." *From "Chemistry and Technology of Leather" edited by Fred O'Flaherty, 1956*

Although English and German tanners were brain tanning as recently as the late 19th and early 20th century, all that remains from stone age Europe are some bone and stone tanning tools. The earliest record of European tanning is in Homer's Iliad (389 f.):

> "The ox hide, which is soaked in fat, is pulled to and fro by men standing in a circle, thus stretching the skin and causing the fat to penetrate into the pores."

One of the things I really like about buckskin is that if we could look back far enough, nearly every one of us would find some ancestor who lived their lives wearing this wonderful garment. It's something we have in common. Getting skins soft was undoubtedly one of the very first arts that ancient humans developed.

Many a campfire has been spent wondering why or who first thought to put brains on a skin? And then stretch it ... dry. Recently I stumbled upon the true story. An Iroquois tale:

> "A stiff deer skin was one day walking around from house to house through an Indian village, frightening everyone it visited. At last it went to the house of a man who was boiling deer's brains for a vomit. He did not propose to be frightened by this mysterious skin out of his house, and therefore he poured the hot water solution of deer's brains upon the stiff skin which at once softened it down, took away from it all power of motion, and flattened it to the floor. The people in fright had been shooting it with arrows. After it was softened they began to pull it and thus resulted the tanned deer skins." *From Lewis H. Morgan's "Iroquois Material Culture", 1855.*

Like most great inventions, it was purely accidental.

Native America

"Na-tuen-de", Apache ,1884

Buckskin was made and used by all of the culture areas of Native North America, from the fishermen of the rainy northwest coast and the caribou hunters of the tundra, to the farmers of the southwest and eastern woodlands. Deerskins were the most commonly tanned, worn and utilized skin because of their durability, softness and availability. They were the basic "fabric" of prehistoric times. Other animal skins were also tanned using variations of the brain tanning process, (buffalo, moose, elk, antelope, caribou, bighorn sheep). Even furs were tanned using brains and woodsmoke, though they were handled differently to prevent the hair from slipping out.

Most of what we know about traditional brain tanning methods comes from the American Indians. There is an extensive record of their tanning processes, written down by anthropologists, explorers and Indians. I have copies of over 100 separate accounts. In this book you will learn about many of the tools, techniques and substances that they used, so that you can try them out yourself.

Colonial America and Europe

Brain tan was the everyday garb of the American Indians when the Europeans first arrived. In Europe the availability of deerskins to the commoner had long since disappeared. Only the aristocracy were allowed to hunt. In the Twenty-Fifth Year of the Reign of King George the Third (1785) came this revision to the Magna Carta of 1215:

> "No man from henceforth shall lose either Life or Member for Killing our Deer: But if any man be taken, and convict for taking of our Venison, he shall make a grievous Fine, if he have anything whereof: and if have nothing to lose, he shall be imprisoned a Year and a Day; and after the Year and Day expired, if he can find sureties he shall be delivered; and if not, he shall abjure the Realm of England."

This version was clearly more lenient than what came before.

The New World, provided a seemingly endless supply of deer. The trade in buckskins, tanned and raw, boomed. Common laborers valued its durability. By the 1750's it was the style among the wealthy of Europe to wear yellow buckskin breeches and gauntlets. It was hunting and riding wear, fashionable in the most elite circles. Customs records indicate that between 1755 and 1773, 2,601,152 lbs. of deerskins were shipped to England from Savannah, Georgia, just one of many ports. Many of these skins had already been brain and smoke tanned by the Creek and Cherokee.

> "Buckskins were universally worn from the tradesmen to those of first rank in the kingdom (England)." *Malachye Postlethewayt, author of "The Universal Dictionary of Trade and Commerce", 1774.*

In America, the pioneers, woodsmen, trappers, soldiers and farmers, anyone who spent time out of the settlements, began to wear buckskin. It was the only fabric that could stand up to the wear and tear of the trail as homespun would snag and tear on the twigs and briars. Plus it could be made at home from a readily available source.

"By 1741, Augusta (Georgia) was, according to one rosy report, thriving 'prodigiously'. The rough little village was declared 'the most flourishing town in the Province.' Augusta's success was largely related to the growing popularity of tanned deerskin for clothing and other uses." *From "Deerskins and Duffels" by Kathryn E. Holland Braund.*

"Deer hides were, in fact, a profitable commercial item and one of the few dependable early sources of income for the settlers. Like the frock, buckskin breeches were first worn by workingmen. In the eighteenth century they were adopted by the English upper classes for hunting, and thus became fashionable. In addition to leggings, moccasins and breeches, buckskin was also used for overalls." *From "Dress for the Ohio Pioneers", edited by Patricia A. Cunningham and Susan Voso Lab.*

When the colonists decided it was time to create their own country and separate from England, the revolutionaries wore buckskin and homespun. It was practical, available and patriotic, for it came from their own land and didn't support British trade. General George Washington ordered thousands of buckskin moccasins and shirts to be made for the troops.

"During the early part of the war a hunting shirt of buckskin or linen, breeches (of buckskin) and gaiters, large brimmed hat, ruffled shirt and black stock was the field service dress recommended by General Washington."

"The final choice of color, which did not materialize until the war's end, resolved into blue coat with red facings and buckskin breeches." *From "How To Make Historic American Costumes" by Mary Evans.*

There was one battalion in particular that was famous for wearing only buckskin: Gen. Daniel Morgan's Riflemen. They were some of the best woodsmen of the time, sent on the more adventurous missions of the American Revolution.

"Like blue jeans today that started as work clothing, were glamorized and then sentimentalized as symbolic of a certain life style, the (buckskin) hunting shirt started as work clothing, was glamorized by its role in the Revolutionary War and then was sentimentalized as symbolic of the intrepid woodsman and explorer." *From "Dress for the Ohio Pioneers"*

Lewis & Clark at Three Forks Montana, a painting by E.S. Paxson

The American Frontier

Buckskin continued to be worn by Indians and frontiers-people alike down through the Civil War. It was worn by the early miners of the California gold rush. It was worn by mountain men, trappers and missionaries. It was worn by the Texas Rangers, and many of those who died in the Alamo. The riders of the Pony Express claimed that it was ideal for cutting cold winds. It was part of the attire of both sides in the battles between the U.S. Cavalry and the Indians. But most of all it was worn by just plain folks.

It was a sign of who was prepared for the rigors of the frontier and who was not. Gustav Dresel, a young German immigrant in the days of the Texas Republic, put it this way:

Jim Bridger, trapper, in a buckskin jacket

"I joined the seven huntsmen, who (were) clad in buckskin from head to foot... My trousers were partially trimmed with buckskin, it is true, and my coat was made of beaverteen (twilled cotton) but they prophesied that even after only a week I should not be able to recognize my exterior because the briars, the thicket, and the wet high grass would harass me so hard. I had traversed the region on the Navasota athwart forest and prairie for four days when rags of my inexpressibles were already suspended from my legs."

Teddy Roosevelt in buckskin hunting gear.

In a letter dated January 16, 1822, Maria Austin wrote her son, Stephen, in Texas:

"I should have exerted myself in

fitting him (brother James) out, agreeable to your wishes—especially in getting him a suit of buckskin. It grieves me whenever I think what a poor outfit he had, so improper for the work he will find necessary to be done."

Did Mother Austin soak her hides in brains? This is not certain. Many during this era used a mixture of soap and lard instead.

The Disappearance of Buckskin....

Buckskin making has always been done by hand. It has never been successfully industrialized. As the industrial revolution penetrated America, durable woven fabrics became available. Made in factories, with all their advantages of material and human exploitation, they were not as durable as buckskin, but they were cheap and much more durable than anything else the machines had churned out. One of these new materials was known as blue jeans, Levi's. Over the year's, Levi's took the place of buckskin in people's wardrobe, until the use and manufacture of buckskin was all but forgotten. It was even discouraged on the reservations. By the turn of the century, most Indians stopped making and wearing brain tan buckskin.

This same period marked the low point of North American deer populations. They had been over hunted for decades by market hunters providing meat and skins to the mining camps, the railroad crews and the rest of the frontier. They were hunted almost as intensely as buffalo, but survived because they lived in diverse habitats coast to coast rather than in giant herds on the open prairie. Their population in the U.S. bottomed out at an estimated 500,000 between the years of 1875 and 1915.

"It (the deer) is so abundant in certain portions of the Pacific Coast that I have heard of market hunters who killed five and six hundred in a season by stalking alone, and it was reported to me in 1874 that over three thousand were slaughtered within a period of five months in a region having an area of less than two hundred miles, and that most of them were sent to market and sold at four cents, or two pence per pound." *John Mortimer Murphy (1879)*

"This ruthless destruction is producing the most disastrous results, for where mule deer were so plentiful in 1868 that they could be seen by the hundred in a march of twenty-four hours, scarcely a dozen could be seen in the same region in 1877." *Same author describing market deer hunting in Montana.*

As the industrial revolution penetrated America, deerskins started to be tanned by the new chrome process. Though the chrome tanned skins were weaker, didn't breath, responded poorly to washing and perspiration, the chrome process made use of inexpensive chemicals and was easy to produce with the new machines. Buckskin tanning is a labor intensive process, lending itself to home-crafting rather than production in a factory.

...And It's Return

Undoubtedly there were some folks somewhere who continued to make buckskin, but the knowledge of its manufacture, once as basic a home industry as soap making, was no longer common. Since 1915 the deer population has rebounded to a healthy 30 million in the U.S. Of the six million deer killed each hunting season only a small percentage ever make it to a tannery. Most are left in the field or tossed into a

Buckskin Slim Schaefer, circa 1970

dumpster. In more recent years various individuals have sought out the knowledge of how to make the buckskin that was described in old woods-lore books and descriptions of the Indians. They sought the aid of Native American friends who remembered some of the old ways. They pieced together what they could from the scanty accounts that were available and tried to find a workable process.

From the backyards, wood lots and reservations of America, this old and nearly lost art was slowly rediscovered. Eventually folks started running into each other and sharing their discoveries, tips and theories, amazed to meet someone else who 'brain-tanned'. Booklets and books were written: *Indian-Tan Buckskin* by Buckskin Slim Schaefer; *Tanning Hides the Sioux Way* by Larry Belitz; *Blue Mountain Buckskin* by Jim Riggs; *Brain-Tan Buckskin* by John McPherson. These books and teachers, among others, set off a renewed interest in the art as people saw the beauty and practicality of buckskin.

Since then many different methods of arriving at that same goal have been discovered or rediscovered. Those of us who brain tan have always been happy to share our new discoveries with one another and as a result we have all gotten better at the art. Much like computers, brain tanning is an art that we are continually improving

our knowledge of as we discover or rediscover better techniques. This book reflects these easier methods.

These days brain tan buckskin is experiencing a much welcomed renaissance. What seemed like an obscure art ten years ago, is now the preferred method for home tanning across America. When I used to tell people what I did for a living I'd say:

> I tan hides using natural oils and woodsmoke, its the old method that people used to use....

Nowadays when I say that same phrase, most people look at me for a second, and then say:

> Oh, you mean you brain tan...

The Nature of Skin

S kin is an amazing material. A brief introduction to its layers and constituents will help you understand what you are doing and why. Skin is traditionally broken down into three layers: the epidermis, the dermis and the hypodermis. The dermis is composed of two layers: the grain (or papillary) layer and the fiber network (or

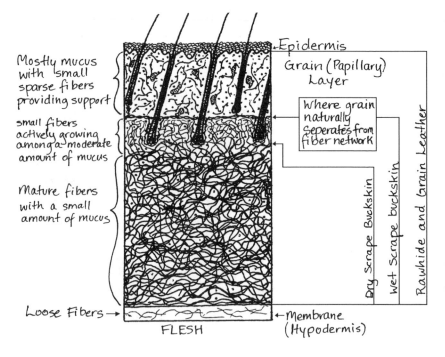

Mostly mucus with small sparse fibers providing support

small fibers actively growing among a moderate amount of mucus

Mature fibers with a small amount of mucus

Loose Fibers →

FLESH

Epidermis

Grain (Papillary) Layer

Where grain naturally seperates from fiber network

Dry Scrape Buckskin

Wet Scrape buckskin

Rawhide and Grain Leather

← Membrane (Hypodermis)

The Layers of Skin

reticular layer). In order to make buckskin we will remove all of these layers except for the fiber network.

Epidermis

The epidermis is the outermost protective layer of the skin. It is much thinner on hairy animals than it is on humans, as the hair serves much the same function of keeping the skin warm and protected from abrasion. It is composed of keratin that is produced in the lower levels. These cells gradually die as they rise to the outer skin. Hair is also keratin and part of the epidermis.

Grain

The grain is also known as the papillary layer. It lies just below the epidermis. This layer contains most of the active living cells of skin. The grain is predominantly composed of mucus with some small thin fibers offering support and structure. This layer is what gives leather its smooth shiny surface.

The Fiber Network

Just below the grain is the fiber network or reticular layer. These fibers are composed of very small spiraling proteins known as collagen. These proteins are twisted around one other in the opposite direction of their spirals, forming little fiber threads. These fiber threads then twist around each other in the opposite direction (this is the same design as rope). The fibers themselves are randomly interwoven into a very strong fabric that is the basis of buckskin and leather.

In the upper reaches of the fiber network new fibers are created by cells know as fibroblasts that receive nutrients from capillaries that run along the junction of the grain and fiber network layers. These fibers are smaller and coated with more mucus than the main body of the fiber network below. The mucus allows the nutrients and amino acids to travel through and feed the growing fibers. The filtering and water binding qualities of this mucus are extremely in-fluential in the tanning process. An intact mucus structure will filter out most of the oils before they can reach the more fibrous interior.

When scraping with a dull tool, the relatively weak grain layer is separated from the top of the fiber network, at the point where these new fibers are being created. When you are scraping you can see that these fibers are quite thin. If you abrade down to deeper levels you can reach the coarser bundles of the main fiber network. These mature fibers have only a small amount of mucus in between them. There is a method of making buckskin in which a sharp tool is used to scrape down to this mature fiber region. Because the oils do not need to penetrate through the fiber growth layer, it is easier to get the oils all the way into the interior. This method is known as dry-scrape.

Membrane

The membrane or hypodermis is where the skin meats the flesh. This membrane allows the skin to move somewhat separately from the underlying muscles. It adds no value to buckskin and is mostly removed.

How Tanning Works

All fabric is composed of woven fibers and skin is no different. What is different is that you don't have to do any weaving. Its already been done . . . by the deer. And the deer is an excellent weaver. Our task is simply to unlock that intricately woven fabric and preserve it in a usable state.

Raw skin if untreated will either dry out and become hard and stiff or remain wet, soft and rot. Our goal is to get the skin to be both soft and dry. There are many ways of accomplishing this that have been developed over the ages, creating different types of leathers and buckskin. Buckskin is made by isolating the fiber network layer of skin. This layer is composed of randomly interwoven fibers that create both strength and flexibility. Then the fibers within this layer are isolated so that they may move freely within their weave, even when dry. Everything that we do is working toward that goal.

Isolating The Fiber Network Layer

All of the skin layers that do not contain the network of fibers must be removed. This is done by laying the hides on a rounded beam, and scraping the layers off with a dull-edged tool. The tool has a distinct enough edge so that you dig in and separate the layers from the fiber core, but dull enough that you don't cut into it. There are three scraping steps. *Fleshing* to remove the mass of meat and fat. *Graining* to remove the hair, epidermis, and grain. And *Membraning* which cleans off the remainder of fleshy and weak fibered tissue. The scraping steps are fairly physical, with graining the most intense. *Bucking* is the traditional term for soaking hides in a solution of wood ashes and water, which causes them to swell. This swelling

A side view of skin after it has been soaked in wood-ashes. The hair to the left is falling out. The grain in the middle is raised, with a distinct drop off to the dermis (fiber network) to the right.

increases the internal cohesion of the grain layer, making it much easier to see and remove (usually one of the hardest steps, especially for beginners). (Note: acids tighten these layers, making them harder to remove, which is why they are used for tanning hides with the hair or fur on, as well as in subsequent steps for grain-on leathers.)

Low-Brow Science

The wood-ash solution is alkaline, meaning that it is full of OH- ions. OH- ions are leading an unbalanced life (they're real negative) and would very much like to bond with a hydrogen atom (H+, which are positive) so that they can become H_2O (which is neutral). In the meantime they hang out with any nearby H_2O, temporarily sharing its H+ atoms. This creates a weak bond between the two causing them to travel around together. In their quest for their own H+ the OH- enter the hide and pull the H_2O in with them, causing the hide to swell.

Cleaning Out The Fiber Network

At some point the interior of the fiber layer must be thoroughly cleaned out. As previously mentioned, the fibers are coated with a protective mucus, also known as the *ground substance*, that filters any substance that enters the skin. This mucus is composed of many molecules (hyaluronic acid, glycosaminoglycans and glycoproteins) that are held together in a system that is shaped like many overlapping bottle brushes. The bottlebrush system is held together by the sharing of hydrogen atoms between different parts.

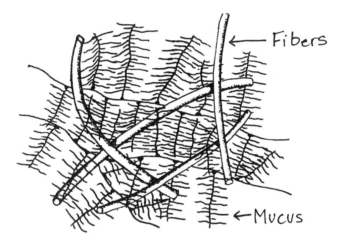

The bottlebrush shape of the mucus allows nutrients and small molecules to flow through the skin, while inhibiting large molecules such as bacteria and tanning oils. The mucus can hold as much as 1000 times its own volume of tissue fluid. Mucus dominates the grain layer and is substantial in the upper growing region of the fiber network. When the hide dries, the mucus structure collapses making the grain layer very thin. Mucus must be broken up or removed for any tanning oils to penetrate.

Hides are also full of water in different levels of bondage: some that can flow freely as tissue fluid, and some that is bound to the fibers and especially to the mucus, by hydrogen bonds. While this mucus-water system is an important protective mechanism in living tissue, in tanning it inhibits lubricants such as brains from reaching the fibers (oil is a large molecule), allowing only water through. All tanning systems, whether intentional or not, rely on disrupting the

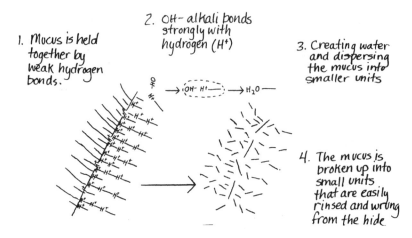

1. Mucus is held together by weak hydrogen bonds.

2. OH- alkali bonds strongly with hydrogen (H+)

3. Creating water and dispersing the mucus into smaller units

4. The mucus is broken up into small units that are easily rinsed and wrung from the hide

How Alkali Break Up the Mucus

mucus-water-fiber bond, and more or less removing the mucus, so that lubricants and tanning substances can reach the fibers and bond with them. This is also key in most other types of hide work such as making glue, parchment, and certain rawhides. There are several known ways to remove the mucus from the hide: soaking in alkali or acids, braining repeatedly, curing dry hides for a year and more. All these methods have their advantages and disadvantages.

Soaking hides in wood ashes or lime has been a very common method both prehistorically and in modern days. As previously mentioned, our overly negative friend the OH- ion is desperately seeking a relationship with a hydrogen atom (H+). The bond that holds the mucus, and mucus-water-fiber system together is the sharing of hydrogen atoms! The heroic OH- ions absorb this hydrogen liberating the mucus, water and fibers from eternal bondage! This allows the mucus to be easily rinsed and wrung out of the hide, leaving the tanner with a clean and open fiber network.

The alkaline soak is simple, predictable and effective. The soaking process requires very little labor, and three days of time. Some other methods will also be presented in the *Tanning Reference* chapter for those circumstances when alkali are not available or appropriate. These methods include multiple wringings and rebraining, curing dry hides, and effectively rebraining hides when necessary.

Rinsing

When all of the scraping steps are complete it is time to thoroughly rinse the mucus and alkali out of the interior of the hide. The alkali are very active and will seek equilibrium with any solution that the hide is placed in. If it is placed in a bucket of water, alkali will leave the hide and enter the water until there are as many alkali in the water as there are in the hide. Then they will stop, and the hide will be full of too many alkali. So the easiest way to rinse out the alkali is by putting the hide in a creek or pond over night. In a creek or pond there is an endless supply of water to whisk the alkali away and absorb more. The other option is to put the hide in a bucket of water with something acidic mixed in, such as vinegar, sour dough or even yeasty beer dregs (the yeasts will keep producing acids, which keep combining with the alkali, making more water).

When the rinsing is done you will notice that all of the swelling has gone down, the hide is stretchy once again, and it has a very dry rather than slimy texture - the mucus is gone. Also you will be able to squeeze air through the hide from the flesh to grain side. This is also a sign that the mucus is gone and the hide more porous.

Wringing

To further prepare the skin for tanning all of the excess water in the hide must be removed. This is accomplished by intensive wringing and squeegeeing. This leaves the fibers damp so that they won't cement together, but with no water between them so that the dressing can slide on in.

Lubricating The Fiber Fabric

When the cleansing, scraping and wringing are complete, we have reduced the skin to nearly pure fibers. These fibers are composed of the protein *collagen* that is the basis of glue (and jello!). When the fibers dry this gluey quality causes them to adhere to one another, creating a hard sheet, known as rawhide. To prevent this adhesion the hide is soaked in emulsified oils. Emulsifiers allow oils to permeate the water with which they are mixed, rather than separating from it. This allows the tanner to coat the fibers with small amounts of lubricating oils without making the hide oily.

Emulsified oils have two ends. One end is a droplet of oil, and the other is a hydrogen atom. The fibers, as you know, had a hydrogen molecule stripped by the alkali. When a fatty acid comes into contact with the empty spot, the H+ end slides into place and the oily end sticks out, helping the fibers to slide along one another. This oily coating helps inhibit the fiber glues from locking the fibers to one another as they dry. Physical manipulation does the rest.

The Great Transformation

As the hide goes from *damp* to dry, the glues start to set up. By stretching the hide, pulling the fibers this way and that, we prevent the glue bonds from setting up and leave the fibers free to move within their weave. The hide must be stretched regularly as the fibers dry layer by layer, from the exterior into the interior. This is the most time consuming and physical step in the tanning process.

Once the hide is dry and soft it will not easily go back to rawhide. However, the hydrogen bond that holds the oils in the fibers is weak and can be broken. If it is exposed to repeated wetting and drying it will stiffen up. Washing can strip the oils right out of the hide.

Preserving The Softness

To better preserve the buckskin in its soft and flexible state, the hide is impregnated with wood smoke. Smoke is known to do two things. It coats the fibers with water resistant resins so that the glues can not be reactivated and it is a highly concentrated gaseous form of natural formaldehyde. This natural formaldehyde changes the actual chemical structure of the collagen fibers, creating cross-links, like little bridges from fiber to fiber that keeps them separated from one another and permanently preserves the soft state of buckskin. These cross links are very strong and can not be washed out. That is one reason smoked buckskin is one of the very few 'leathers' that can be washed. You will notice that once smoked the hide feels very different when wet. It has a drier texture and most of the water is easily squeezed out.

Smoking also raises the temperature that the fibers can be exposed to before they break down, and makes them less susceptible to bacteria and rot. Most leathers are based on acidic chemical tanning. They are extremely stable when exposed to heat or bacteria. Chrome tans can even be boiled. However, these acid bonds are easily weakened by alkaline fluids such as soap, detergent, sweat and milk. Smoked buckskin is not broken down by sweat or soap and this is another reason why it is ideal for clothing.

Skinning

Skinning is a straight forward endeavor if you follow the body's built in guidelines. This is because protective membranes naturally separate the skin and muscle tissue from one another. Simply make the initial cuts, and then *pull* the skin off, as if you are removing the deer's coat. When you peel the skin, it easily separates from the meat along these membranes. After getting a clean start, there is little risk of tearing the skin or the meat. So all you need to do is use your hands and body weight to pull and pry the skin from the deer. It is generally a five to fifteen minute process.

The biggest mistake you can make is trying to cut the hide off with your knife. When you use a knife to slice the hide from the deer you *inevitably* violate these layers, making the whole job harder. Once the meat is cut into, you are no longer working with the natural division between meat and hide. You usually end up removing large chunks of meat, as well as putting cuts and holes in the hide. These cuts (also called scores) and holes open up and enlarge easily, increasing the amount of work at every stage of the tanning process.

The membranes that encase the meat also protect it from flies and deer hair. When you cut into the meat you create moist and protected habitats for flies to lay their eggs in. If you peel the skin, the muscle layers remain intact, the outer membranes dry out, and flies will not lay their eggs. For some reason, most modern hunters do not know this and that makes finding well-skinned hides a real challenge. There are absolutely no advantages to knifing a skin off. It is not faster!

How To Skin

Hanging the deer makes it easy to use your body weight to pull the skin off. It also assures that the meat will stay clean. You can either hang it from the neck or from the legs. Most people prefer one way or the other. I like them both. Deer should be hung using strong ropes (I had one fall on me once when the rope broke. The antler tines hit my forehead. Those things hurt!). Do it within a few hours of the deer's death and it will peel off especially easily. Make sure your knife is sharp, and proceed as follows

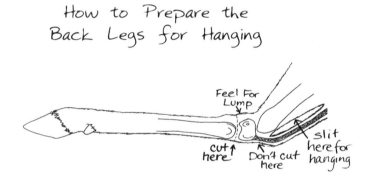

Cut skin and tendons around the joint, then snap it over your leg.

To hang a deer by its back legs, find the large tendon that connects the lowest leg segment with the rest of the leg. Poke a hole in between that tendon and the leg bone. Use your fingers to feel the lump that is created by the double-jointed bone. Then sever the lower leg at the lower of the two joints as illustrated.

Tip: If you want to get better hides tell your friends who hunt about good skinning techniques, or post a flyer around town.

Skinning Cuts & Hide Shape

Where you make your cuts up the legs and across the chest & groin will effect the final shape of your hide. The method we showed in the first edition of this book (and the way most hunters and butchers do it) leaves you with a significant narrow area under the front legs, and puts very weak loin skin along the bottom edge that is prone to tearing when you soften on a frame.

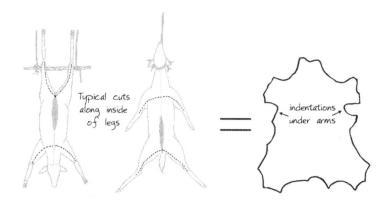

If you shift your cuts to the line where the white and brown hair meet (forward on the front legs, and backward on the back legs) you end up with a more useable, rectangular shape that you see in many old hides. This really gets valuable when you are making something.

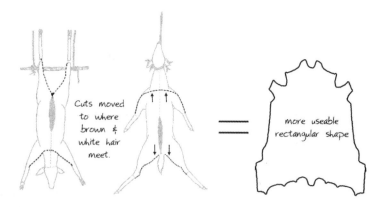

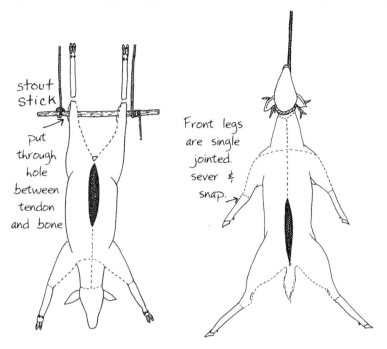

Make the incisions as shown. Once you've made the initial incisions, put that knife down. Then use your hands and body to pull, yank, and pry the skin from the deer.

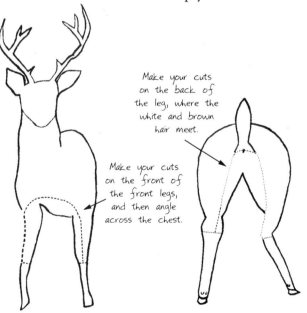

Getting a clean start: use fingertips and thumbs to separate the hide from the meat. Notice how clean and encased both the meat and hide are.

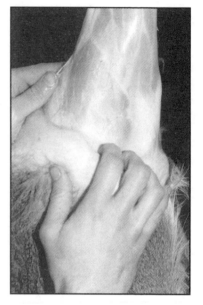

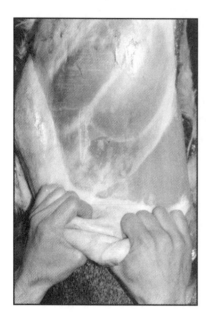

Once you've gotten a good start, grab the hide with your hands and pull. You can also push your thumbs, fist and elbows in-between the skin and meat to release areas that are sticking.

There will be a very thin layer of meat that wants to come off with the hide. This is the muscle that the deer uses to twitch flies off of its back. Very few people eat this meat because it is so thin and membraney. It is easily fleshed off later, so let it come off with the hide.

Use your body weight to help pull.

Removing the Brains

Deer conveniently come with just enough brains to tan their own skin. If you are planning to tan the hide right away, the simplest place to store the brains is in the intact skull. To remove the brains from the skull you first need to cut away the skin that covers the area between the eyes and the back of the antlers (on does just go to where the antlers would be). Then use a hacksaw to make a V shaped cut into the skull. The antlers can be used as a lever to remove the cut bone. A messier but equally effective alternative is to smash this section of skull with a stone. Be careful not to cut yourself on bone shards. Once the skull is open use a spoon, fingers or straw to remove all of the brains. Protect the brains from flies.

Sinew

Along either side of the backbone is a long flat band of sinew. This sinew is made up of many individual threads that have a myriad of practical uses. We use them as thread to sew the holes closed in our buckskin. Sinew and hide glue applied together to wood surfaces creates a very strong natural 'fiberglass' that is used for binding ar-

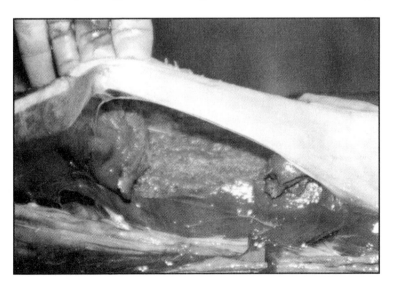

rowheads and feathers onto arrows, for backing bows and anything else where a strong binding is needed.

You usually need to peel away a thin layer of flesh adjacent to the backbone to expose the sinew. Then use your fingers or a *dull* knife to pry the sinew up from the underlying meat. Work the sinew free all the way up into the shoulders and down toward the rump. You can get a really long strip if you follow it all the way. Up by the shoulders the end of the sinew comes free by itself, but down by the rump you need to cut it off. Scrape the sinew free of any meat bits with your knife held *perpendicularly* to the sinew. This can be done while it is still attached to the body, or afterwards.

Obtaining Hides

There are lots of free and cheap hides available every hunting season and frequently in-between. With a little effort you should be able to find all that you could ever want. However it *is* a bit trickier finding hides that haven't been knifed up in the skinning. Tanning hides that have been skinned well is a joy. Tanning knifed up skins takes longer in nearly every stage, and the finished product is not nearly as good. Go to extra lengths to get good skins. If you are buying deerskins, it is always worth a few extra bucks for really good ones.

While this book is geared particularly toward the tanning of deer hides, you can also use these same methods to tan elk, antelope, moose, goat, Big Horn sheep and buffalo. I haven't tanned any elk and I rarely hear anything good about it. They are much more work to tan and because of their fiber structure, they are weaker and wear out faster than deer. This is just a relative comparison. Elk leather is beautiful, large, thick and perfectly fine for many applications. Moose on the other hand has the fiber quality of deer but the thickness of moose. They are particularly great for moccasins. Antelope and big-horn sheep are renowned for being uniformly thin. They will make lightweight, comfortable dresses and summer clothing.

Where to get good skins

Deer you hunt yourself. What could be more satisfying than pulling on a deerskin jacket from deer that fed you and your family? Obviously do not hunt deer just to get more skins. There are a zillion out there going to waste.

Friends who hunt. If you know lots of folks who hunt, just tell them you want the skin, and most would love to give it to you. Have a handout to give them on good skinning techniques or offer to skin for them. (Feel free to xerox the pages on skinning from this book).

Roadkills. More than 300,000 deer are hit annually in the United States. You can get lots of free, perfectly skinned hides, with no bullet holes. It may be illegal in your area, so check it out. Skin the deer, remove any meat you will use, and return the carcass to somewhere that the critters can get to it safely, away from the road.

Take Basic Precautions

Rotting, smelly hides can give you an infection or blood poisoning real fast. If you handle any questionable hides, wash up thoroughly afterwards with disinfectant soap and keep an eye on any cuts or sores. If you notice an unusual amount of swelling, or red streaks going from your cuts toward the chest, see a physician immediately.

Skinning stations. Set up a free skinning station along a road that many hunters will use. This is especially effective during peak hunting weekends, and in regions where a large number of tags have been issued for an area with only a few main access roads. You can also offer to do it at your home, and advertise.

Roadside barrels. My friend Jim Riggs puts out two or three barrels every year with a sign that reads "hides and heads". Luckily most people interpret this to mean deer and elk. He gets all of the free hides and brains that he can use. If you try this be prepared to deal with some gross hides, yellow jackets and trash. You will also get a lot of real crappy hides, but you will find some gems. Jim always wishes that the good skinners would autograph their hides.

Local butchers who do game processing. Look in the yellow pages under meat. There you will find a list of all local butchers who do game processing. Call them and ask them how much they charge, how many skins they get a season, etc.

They will all tell you that they do a really great skinning job. Most of them don't. It's really hard to see knife marks in frozen or wet salted hides. So check out a sample of their work before you make any big purchases. Either buy one frozen or salted hide or check out a freshly skinned hide if that is possible. Rinse the salt out of the salted hide. On the flesh side look for knife marks. These will appear as cuts in the skin or the meat. It is preferable to have none, but this, sadly, is rare.

As long as only one person is doing the skinning, the quality or lack of, will be consistent. If there are only a few knife marks on the edges and none in the middle, this is good. If their are knife marks in the middle of the hide, this is the sign of a hide slasher. Avoid these. I shop around for the best skinners, and make a deal to get every-thing they skin that deer season. Tell them that you only want their hides, and not ones that hunters bring in.

Sometimes you can get a butcher to change his skinning prac-tices so that he pulls the skin off (see *Skinning* p. 38). This is rare, but worth the effort and paying a little more for it. A typical price for a deerskin from the butchers in 2004, is from four to ten dollars. Even better is to get a job skinning for a butcher during the opening weekend of deer season, and get the hides for free.

Hide dealers and tanneries. Most big towns have someone who buys hides from hunters. If yours does, ask that person to put aside the very best. Offer to pay a dollar or two more than they are currently getting, for their best ones. Ask them to put aside twice as many as you actually want. Then go through the pile and pick out the best. This is a bit of a Russian roulette since it is hard to see knife marks through the salt. If you explain to the dealer that you want the hides with the least knife marks, and then you go through them yourself, you will mostly get good ones.

Become a deer hide buyer and dealer. If your area doesn't have a hide buyer, you could become that person. Find out where the closest tannery is, and how much they will pay you per hide. Then buy hides at prices that will make it worth your while. A common deal is to offer free leather gloves in exchange for hides. Hunters like this. These gloves are available wholesale for two to three bucks from Sullivan's Gloves, 1315 S.E. Armour Rd, Bend Oregon 97702. (541) 382-3092. You need to order 60 to get the wholesale price. Advertise at hunting shops, etc.

You will be surprised how many you get, especially if you do it year after year. Most hunters would like to see their hides get used, just out of ethics. This way you can pick out the very best hides when they are fresh, plus make money reselling the others to the tannery. Have a flier, that illustrates proper skinning techniques. Offer more mula for peeled hides.

By buying hides directly from hunters, you will not be encouraging folks to go out and kill deer to sell you the skin. The going rate for deerskins is so low it would never be worth it. Rather, you are just giving them a little incentive to get their skin to someone who will use it, instead of leaving it in the woods or the trash.

Storing Hides

You want to store hides so that they are in optimum condition for tanning: *uniformly moist*, and protected from rot, dogs, ringtails, bears and bugs.

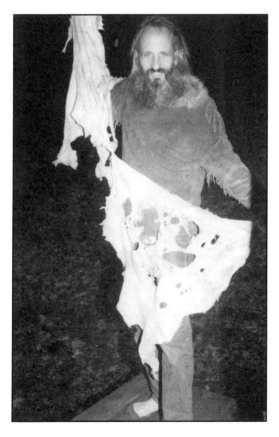

This hide wasn't stored so good.

How to Store Hides

Freeze

Roll hide up in tight bundle, tie, put in plastic bag, and freeze indefinitely. You can flesh first to reduce volume. If you have the freezer space, this is the easiest way to go.

Wet-salt

Lay hide out flat with the flesh side facing up. Spread fine salt over the entire surface, all the way out to the edges. Don't skimp, salt is cheap. To salt the next hide, lay it directly on top of the first, and so on. Allow the salt to soak in overnight. Store in cool place with *no air flow, so they won't dry out.* Use tight plastic and wooden containers. Salt will rust metal, which will then stain the hide. One or two hides will fit in a five gallon plastic bucket, while a big pile can be put into a garbage can. After one week drain any water that has accumulated at the bottom of the container. Will store at least one year. This is the most practical method for people who tan a lot of hides.

Storing salted hides in tarps or other permeable containers causes them to dry slowly over time. The more they dry the harder they will be to scrape later. Even if they feel damp and pliable they may still have dried enough to affect scraping. Wet-salted hides should feel as loose as when they first came off of the deer.

The only way to really screw this up is by storing salted hides directly on the ground. Somehow the ground causes the hides to rot over time.

Scrape Fresh and Then Dry

To do this, you must flesh, buck, grain and rinse. Then you can dry the hide out and store it indefinitely. Drying unscraped hides makes them considerably harder to scrape later. So, if you take them through the grain scraping stage and then dry them, you are not creating any unnecessary work for yourself. It takes an experienced tanner about an hour's work to get a hide to this point (not including soaking time). It might take a beginner four or five hours. Use *The Basic Method* p. 67.

Drying Hides Before Graining Makes it Harder

For four years, I fleshed and dried my hides for storage. Many brain-tanners do this. This is fine for dry-scraping. For wet-scraping this can make it much harder to remove the grain. Drying shrinks the grain and causes it to adhere tightly to the fiber core. When re-soaked, it doesn't reconstitute fully.

> *Think of a dried apple...when reconstituted, no matter how long it soaks or is manipulated, is it ever as soft, full and luscious as a fresh apple?*

No...and the same is true of hide grain. The grain will never swell and loosen to be as easy to remove as on fresh hides.

There are however a couple of exceptions to this rule. Hides that have been stored dry for more than a year will grain fairly easily. Hides that have been stored dry for a few years are exceptionally easy to grain and soften. In fact there is no need to do the bucking or rinsing steps. The aging process has an effect similar to the alkali, causing the mucus in the grain layer to break down. This allows the dressing to easily enter and prepare the hide for softening. So if you have some old hides out in the shed, soak them up in plain water for a day or two and go at it.

Using the bucking process as illustrated in *The Basic Method* makes dried hides scrape much easier than they otherwise do, so I don't discourage it as much as I did in the past. If you do not have an environmentally responsible way to dispose of salt, no freezer, and you're tanning a lot of hides, this may be your only option. Give the hide a very thorough fleshing job because any fat left on the hide will rot and weaken it. Dry in a fairly warm place so that the hide dries before it rots. Check the edges periodically as they have a tendency to curl up and hold moisture in.

Hides dried hair-on need to be protected from bugs, especially once spring rolls around. The omnipresent nasty hide beetles will infest and chew holes in any skins stored dry with the hair on, unless the hides are stored where the bugs can't get them, or in a smoky spot. The hide beetles don't like the flavor of smoky hides. These cruel bugs also don't like to munch hairless hides. This is another good reason to scrape the grain off of your hides before drying them. Getting a hide to this point only takes about one hour or two of work for an experienced tanner. This won't be too much work at once unless you are tanning 30+ hides. In that case you have to deal with the realities of mass production, however you see fit.

Another Option

You can soak your hides in the alkali buck and rinse them before storing; then store them using any of these methods. The advantage of this is that you can make just one batch of solution and put all of your hides through the bucking process at once. Then your hides will be immediately ready to scrape whenever you are, rather than having to wait for them to go through the bucking process. The disadvantage is that you don't get the easier scraping that swollen hides provide. It also takes considerably longer for the hide to rinse: about 48 hrs. in moving water. I encourage you to leave them in the buck and in the rinse a little longer than necessary, to make *sure* that the whole batch is fully treated and ready. You might as well since you are not in a hurry to scrape them, and it doesn't create any more work for you.

Tools You Will Need

The tools of this trade are easy to find and make. You probably have most of them on hand already. You can also order the most crucial tools from *Traditional Tanners Supply* (see p. 238). You should have all of your tools ready to go before you start each stage of the tanning process. The chapter *Nature's Tools* describes how to make and use a wide selection of stone, wood, bone and shell tools. You might try these after you have a hide under your belt.

The Scraper

Along with the beam, this is a very important tool. You want a flat steel bar, with a distinct edge to it, and comfortable handles. The main variables are how well the tool maintains its distinct edge and how comfortable it is to hold and use. There are many things that will work.

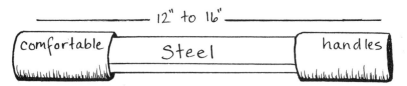

Steel is the material of choice for modern hide-tanners because it holds its edge the best. Some steels holds their edge better than others. My favorite scraper is a **Mill-planer**. These are used by logging mills to plane one by twelves. Local mills often have old ones that they will give you. They are also sometimes available from machine shops and various folks listed in the resource directory at the back of this book. They hold their edge for a very long time. I re-work mine once every fifty hides or so.

You can also use **leaf springs** from cars. You will need to grind an edge on them. They are made of a softer steel, and you will have to re-work the edge every few hides.

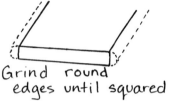

Grind round edges until squared

Drawknives are the tool of choice for many who scrape on the upright pull beams:

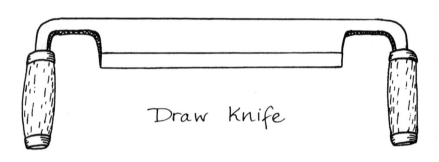

Draw Knife

You can use any piece of steel that meets the shape and edge requirements. In a pinch, I have used angle irons and railroad ties.

Comfortable Handles

Comfortable and stable handles are crucial for pleasant and effective scraping. Being able to put a lot of force into your scraping is very important. This is difficult to do with sore, blistering hands. The keys to good handles are roundness and size. The rounder your handles are, the less force is focused on any one point of your hand. If your handles are too small they also tend to dig in. It is very distracting if your handles slide around, so make them secure. Bicycle handles are just about perfect.

Quick and easy handles can be made from heater hose, available at hardware stores. Get the size that will just barely slide onto the end of your tool when you flatten the hose. It should have enough grip that it won't slide back off, even in use. These handles work

Tool Checklist

For Scraping

❑ Hide

❑ Scraping Beam

❑ Scraper

❑ 20-30 gallon plastic garbage can, or wooden barrel

❑ Two to three gallons of wood ash, 2 oz KOH or one lb. hydrated lime

For Dressing and Softening

❑ Dressing

❑ Wringing stick (an old axe handle or similarly sized, strong smooth stick)

❑ Softening tool (I recommend a cable for your first hide)

❑ Sewing thread and needle (optional, see *Sewing Holes* p. 103)

For Smoking

❑ Glue (elmer's, wood, or hide)

❑ Smoking skirt (get a pair of large sized old jeans from a thrift store, or a two foot by four foot piece of canvas. See p. 126)

❑ *Smoking* material (see p. 128)

quite well though they are not ideal. Our hands definitely get sore if we are scraping several hides for the first time in a while. Replace hose when they start to wear out on the inside.

Other good handles I have seen have been made of wood and of antler. For antler you need two pieces that have a pith that is bigger than your scraper. This pith should be dense and hard. Old weathered antler will not work. Soak the antler overnight. Then, bring to a simmer for twenty minutes. This will soften the pith, so that you can push the metal up into it. When the antler dries, the pith will lock the antler to the metal. This works best if the steel has a narrower section and then bulges at the end. Boil the antler for the shortest amount of time you can and still have it work. Usually you can push the steel in part of the way and then pound it the rest with a wooden mallet. File down the antler's surface until it is smooth.

The Scraper's Edge

Having a proper edge on your scraper is extremely important! Too sharp and you will cut your hide to bits. Really dull and graining will be impossible. The tool's edge can be square or beveled as long as it has an edge. You want a distinct edge, but *not a sharp one*. You want an edge that will grip the bottom of the grain layer as you push it off. The edge should also be *very straight with no nicks*, so that no

Tool must have an edge
They can be squared or beveled

whet stone

Edge must be smooth with no nicks or chipped edges

Tool Edges Should Be Dulled
(even if they are square)

grain is missed or the fiber core scratched.

It is easiest to sharpen the tool with a stone or grinding wheel and then purposely dull it with your sharpening stone. I would greatly encourage you to err on the side of a bit too dull rather than a bit too sharp. It is never worth marring the finished hide in exchange for slightly easier scraping. There are other ways to make scraping easier if this is necessary (see p. 145 in *Tanning Reference*).

It's not too sharp if:

* You can run your finger along the edge, with absolutely no possibility of cutting yourself.

* You can clearly see the roundedness of the *very* edge.

* It doesn't make holes or cuts in your hide.

A test I picked up from Steven Edholm is to try to shave your thumbnail. If you can then it is too sharp.

It's not too dull if:

* There is an edge.

* It only looks *slightly* rounded.

* It works.

Scraping Beams

There are two different ways to set up a beam. A **waist beam** is propped up so that one end is at the height of your abdomen and the other end is on the ground. An **upright beam** is leaned against a tree or wall. A pushing motion is used with the former and a pulling motion with the latter. Instructions in this book will be geared toward the waist beam because that is what I use, although they can be easily applied to the upright style. Most people use whatever style they first learned on. There does not seem to be any cut and dry advantages to either setup. I would assume that the waist style allows you to use your body weight more effectively, but I've really never given the other setup a fair shake. Your scraping beam is one of your most important tools and setting up a good one will help make everything go smoothly.

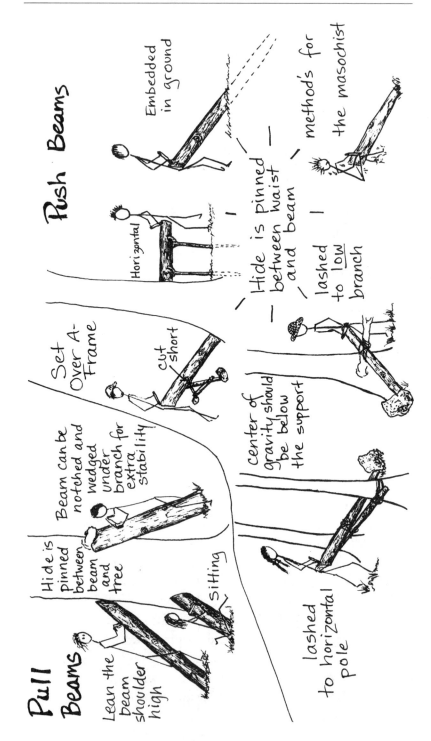

Push Beams

Embedded in ground

methods for the masochist

Horizontal

Hide is pinned between waist and beam

lashed to low branch

Set Over A-Frame

cut short

center of gravity should be below the support

Pull Beams

Hide is pinned between beam and tree

Beam can be notched and wedged under branch for extra stability

sitting

lashed to horizontal pole

Lean the beam shoulder high

How To Make A Beam

These are the important characteristics of a good beam setup:

Material. You can get away with almost any wood type, but certain woods are easier to maintain. Try to select a wood that doesn't develop cracks or splinters easily. Soft deciduous trees work well. I've used cottonwood and big-leaf maple. Some folks like birch. If you harvest a living tree for your beam, you must dry it slowly so that it doesn't crack too much.

The working surface is an approximately six inch wide by two foot long area, located at the end of the log nearest your waist. Your working surface should be:

(A) *Smooth.* No cracks (you can get away with tiny ones), knots, lumps, or dips. You want it as perfectly smooth as you can get it. It is best to start with a section of log that is naturally smooth.

(B) *Rounded.* Any flat spots will make effective scraping difficult to impossible on that spot. The more sharply rounded it is the easier it is to scrape the grain off the hide, but the more you need to move your skin around. A good balance to start with is a nicely rounded beam six to eight inches in diameter. If you find scraping difficult, use a narrower beam.

Length. As long as you are tall is a good length for a beam.

Make it stable! Any movement your beam makes when you scrape, is energy diverted from the task at hand. You want all of your force to be transferred into scraping off those layers. If your beam moves while you are scraping, stop and firm it up.

More on Beams

Waist Beam. The shorter your waist beam, the steeper the angle it sits at, and the steeper your stoop as you scrape. The longer it is, the more horizontal it is and the less you bend over. I like a compromise between portability and comfortable scraping.

Neck beams. The neck is the hardest section of a hide to scrape. It is often advantageous to use a very narrow beam. The narrower and more steeply rounded your beam, the less contact there is on the hide between your scraper and the beam. This concentrates your

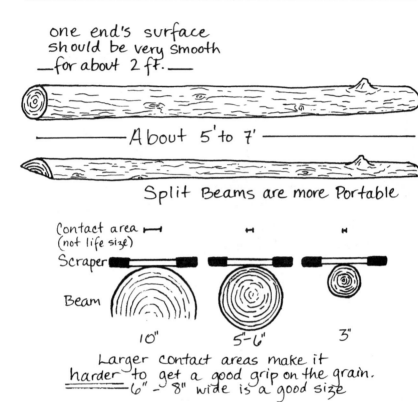

one end's surface should be very smooth —for about 2 ft.—

——— About 5' to 7' ———

Split Beams are more Portable

Contact area ⊢⊣ (not life size)

Scraper

Beam

10"   5-6"   3"

Larger contact areas make it harder to get a good grip on the grain. —6" - 8" wide is a good size

force into a much smaller area, and allows you to more effectively remove the grain. You will however have a smaller working surface, and have to move your hide around more often.

Neck grain that was brutal to scrape on a typical beam, becomes relatively easy on a neck beam. Having a neck beam handy, can make the difference between a pleasant scrape, or an agonizing one. Though not always necessary, we always have one on hand.

Beams unlimited. Any rounded working surface at a comfortable height, of any smooth material will work. Some folks swear by six inch PVC plastic piping. I've used five gallon buckets stacked and then leaned over a fence, using the side of the top bucket as the scraping surface. Wood however is the ideal material. It has just the right amount of give to prevent any tearing of the skin, and it is easy to re-smooth any gouges made into it.

Beam maintenance. Don't leave your beam out in the weather for long periods of time like we do. When not generally in use, store it in a dry, shaded spot. Otherwise, cracks will develop and worsen, ruining your beam. Periodically remove gouges in the wood, and re-round any spots that have become flattened by your scraper.

Wood Ash, Lye or Lime

Wood Ash

What you are after is white ash, not charcoal, though it's harmless if your ash has some charcoal mixed in with it. All ash works, but the strength of the ash from different woods varies. Soft woods create more ash but the ash is weaker, so you need more. Hard woods create less ash, but it's strong, so you need less. Collect at least two gallons of hard wood or three gallons of soft wood ash for your first hide. For each additional hide collect one and a half gallons. It's nice to have more than you need. A lot of trees do not fall into these unrealistically neat and tidy categories, so just get whatever ash is available and we'll work with it from there.

If you plan on tanning more than one batch of hides you can reuse your ash solution and wring excess out of the hides as you remove them. This will cut down on ash consumption to a gallon per hide or less. Store ash dry, as rain will leach out the alkalinity. If you don't burn wood, you can usually find a brick-oven bakery or potters who will regularly produce considerable quantities. Avoid ash that is full of trash.

The old term for soaking something in wood ashes was *bucking*. Linen was bucked to bleach it. Once a year a family's clothes would be bucked to give them a really deep cleaning. The connection to making buckskin seems pretty clear, so that's what we'll call it.

Wood-ash Substitute

The best substitute for wood-ash lye is the man-made version of the active ingredient: **potassium hydroxide** (KOH). It works exactly like the lye you would make from wood-ashes, and is real easy to use. We use about 8 ounces to 20 gallons of water and four hides (or two ounces to five gallons and one hide, etc.). KOH is available from soap-making suppliers as well as from *Traditional Tanners Supply* (see p. 239). In pioneer days a version of this known as 'pearl-ash' was made by dehydrating wood-ash lye and was traded and sold throughout the colonies. Nowadays it is made by running electricity through potassium rich soil known as potash.

Red Devil lye

Red Devil (sodium hydroxide) is available at most grocery stores and also works. One detraction is that it makes the hides slippery, and a bit harder to scrape as a result. This effect can be relatively minor, or it can be a pretty big hassle. Use six to eight ounces of Red Devil brand lye (available in the household cleanser section of any grocery store) to 2/3rds of a 30 gallon plastic trash can. If the hides are slippery, soak them in plain water until its they're easier to handle (usually a dip will do) before scraping, and/or place a piece of textured fabric – like a towel scrap – between you and the hide when scraping. Is it still natural tanning? Or the devil in a can? You decide.

Use caution with either of these lyes, particularly before they are mixed with water (that is when they can burn you), and store out of the reach of children. If you wait a few extra days before disposing, the lye will significantly weaken and be less likely to harm plant life. Usually the grass grows taller and greener, though if you poured too much too often in the same place it would likely kill the plants. All of the information we've found so far from water and fisheries specialists indicate that it's OK to leach these lyes from hides in waterways, as long as quantities are limited, but I can't guarantee this.

Lime

Lime may also be used to create an alkaline soak. It is available at most farm, garden or feed stores. It is cheap and easy to use. The type of lime that you want is called "hydrated". It combines with water quickly and easily. One advantage of lime is that you can not make too strong of a mixture; it reaches saturation in water at just about the right strength. One detraction is that if you leave your hides in it for a long time (i.e. weeks) your hides will come out tighter and less stretchy. This quality is excellent for moccasins, or bags, but not so appealing in a loin cloth. This gets more pronounced the longer hides soak in lime. Lime also tends to be more irritating to the skin than lye as the result of sharp calcium particles. Given the choice, I prefer either wood-ashes or KOH to lime any day.

Dressings (Choose One)

Emulsified oils are used to condition and soften the hide. An emulsified oil uniformly saturates water rather than separating from it. This quality allows the tanner to lubricate the fibers with oils without getting the hide oily. Milk is the classic example of an emulsified oil, and all of these dressings will look milky when they are in use.

Brains

Brains were the traditional dressing of primitive peoples all over the world, and what I have the most experience with. If you don't have the brains that came with the hide, you'll need to get someone. Any brains will do. You can buy beef or pork brains at the butcher shop or through the meat department at the grocery. Look under "meat" in the yellow pages and call around. Some places carry them; especially if there is a Mexican population (many eat brain tacos). If nobody has them on hand, most places can order them. Always start with, "Hello, I'm looking for some brains," or "Hello, do you have any brains?" A typical price in 2002 is anywhere between 80 cents and $2.25 per pound. You need about half a pound per hide, but get at least a pound. Brains rot very quickly. Store brains frozen, canned or dried. Instructions for drying brains are in *Nature's Tools* p. 164.

Eggs

I have tanned and watched many others tan perfectly nice hides with eggs. They were even occasionally used by some Native American tribes. Use a dozen healthy chicken eggs per hide.

Soap and Oil

Natural pure soaps can be used as an emulsifier for oils. Use animal fat or olive oil (other vegetable oils might work; I've just never tried them). I've done this method with pure neat's foot oil which is available at feed stores. Many pioneers used soap and lard. A lot of American Indians currently use Ivory soap in their tanning. I've also watched various people use olive oil, shortening or bear fat. I would avoid tallow as the wax might get in the way. Use a 1/4 of a bar of soap with 1/4 cup oil per hide.

Cable

Cables are extremely effective stretching tools. You can work the hide more intensely on a cable than any other way. They are also great for working the edges. The most effective version is 1/8 to 1/4 inch "aircraft cable" available at some hardware stores. Get a piece four to five feet long and two cable clamps that are designed for that diameter cable. Cable kits are also available through *Traditional Tanners Supply* (see p. 238). In a pinch you can use rope, though they are not as effective and wear out fast.

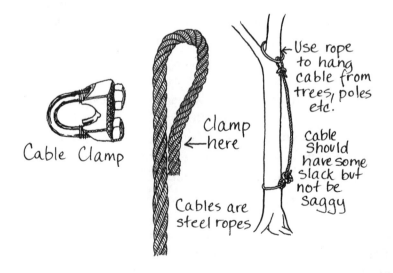

Cable Clamp

Clamp
←here

Cables are
steel ropes

←Use rope
to hang
cable from
trees, poles
etc.

cable
should
have some
slack but
not be
saggy

Pumice

Pumice will impart a very silky texture to the hide surface. I also like its ability to remove large quantities of membrane fast. It is a very light, porous and abrasive volcanic rock. You can get pumice through most rock shops, some hardware stores, by harvesting your own (It can be quite exhilarating harvesting your materials at 10,000 feet up a volcano), or from *Traditional Tanners Supply* (see p. 239). Get a piece a little smaller than a baseball. Pumice should be gritty and moderately hard. If you ever notice it cutting lines into your buckskin, discard it for a better piece. Do not bother with pumice that crumbles easily or that is really soft.

The Basic Method

This basic method is the simplest way that I know of to produce excellent buckskin. The instructions are deliberately limited to what you need to do with little discussion of the whys and wherefores, except when it will really help. This is done so that you are not afflicted by information overload, and can easily find and reference instructions as you go. There is a tanning reference section following the basic method for when you have further questions.

Buckskin tanning is a simple but precise art. These instructions tell you very specifically what to do, when and how. The words are chosen quite carefully, and the methods and techniques are well tested. Follow them and you will make some really soft and beautiful buckskin. When you have a good feel for this, have made some soft stuff, go ahead and tinker if you like. By then, you will have pocketed a simple method, a warm and cozy home that you can always return to after a tanning adventure.

Tanning is a very tactile and organic art. There are a multitude of unpredictable variables that can come into play. Thankfully, buckskin is a very forgiving teacher. It is fairly hard to ruin your hide. You might have to redo steps, making the process considerably longer, but you will still tan some really nice buckskin. I'll try to tell you in the text what can go wrong and how to compensate. I've probably made most of the mistakes that exist (though I'm sure to find more), but have only completely ruined two hides. There are four ways that you can really ruin a hide:

* Allowing it to rot.
* Allowing the hide to get too hot (over 120 degrees) - usually by using too hot of a dressing solution.
* Scraping with a really sharp tool.
* Catching the hide on fire while smoking. This is generally the result of the smoker deciding to go get a cheese sandwich and leaving the smoking hides unattended.

Buckskin making is a physical process, especially the scraping and softening steps. Do them when you are in the mood to do some moderate exercise and it will feel great. Cheaper than the gym with great results to boot.

Once your hide is wet and in process, you should not go on any extended vacations until it has reached one of the storage stages indicated on the next page. Try to finish the step that you are on in each sitting and the scraping steps within the course of a couple of days. Rinse it, store it, and then go to Barbados. Properly stored hides can be left for long periods of time. Years even. Though I doubt you'll be able to wait so long!

Getting ready

Before starting you need to take your hides out of storage and get them as soft and flexible as they were when fresh. If your hide is fresh then you are ready to go. Frozen hides need to be thawed. With this method, salted hides don't need to be rinsed out before starting. The salt gets rinsed out along with the alkali in the 'rinsing' step. They should, however, be soaked overnight in a barrel of water to rehydrate them. (For methods that don't use alkali and subsequent rinse, salt should be thoroughly rinsed out ahead of time soaking the hide in a barrel overnight, with water trickling through.)

Fully and partially dried hides should be soaked for 24 hours and refleshed in order to open up the pores. Hides that have not significantly dried in storage *and* do not have a thick layer of flesh, can be put straight into the buck and fleshed afterwards. Anything thicker than a half inch needs be to removed before bucking.

Organizing Your Time

This is meant as a simple chart to help you plan your time. You can take breaks at any time except when actually softening or smoking. Long term breaks can be taken at the stages indicated. Times given on the right are approximate. There are many variables (such as you, your kids, telephones, watching birds). Like many things in life, it's more fun if you don't think about the time.

Fleshing	scraping (moderately physical)	**10 to 40 min.**
Soaking		**~three days**
Graining	scraping (physical)	**1 to 5 hrs.**
Rinsing		**overnight**
Acidifying		**15 min to overnight**
Membraning		**10 to 30 min.**

can dry or freeze hides for storage . . . .

Wringing		
Dressing	light work	**20 to 60 min.**

can dry or freeze hides for storage . . . .

Wringing	vigorous	
Softening	exercise	**2 to 5 hrs.**

hide is dry and can be stored . . . .

Making the Sack	setup and	
Smoking	monitoring	**1 to 3 hrs.**

The longer times are approximately what you should expect your first time. The shorter times are how long it takes when you have some experience, and the hide is cooperative.

Fleshing

The goal of this step is to remove the meat, fat, and lumpy membrane. Put on some clothes that you don't mind getting grimy and/or wear some sort of apron. Some folks just tie a trash bag around their waists. Make sure your tool has the appropriate edge. See p. 56.

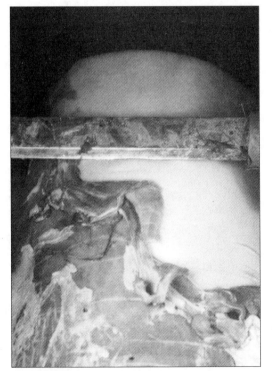

How to:

Lay hide on beam flesh side up, with part of the hide hanging over the upper end of the beam. Press abdomen against beam, pinching hide in place.

Scrape off a section of meat and fat by pushing tool down into hide, forward and off. Scrape from cleaned sections into the areas that have not yet been fleshed, using your tool like a plow.

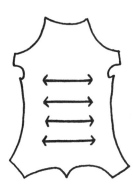

You will notice that the flesh comes off easier scraping from belly to belly rather than neck to tail.

the *very* edge of skin.

Keep adjusting the skin, so that the section you are working on is right in front of you. There is no need to be fussy. You only need to remove the meat and fat. The membrane is easier to get in a later step. Just go over the hide removing everything obvious. If it's not obvious, it's not important.

Hides are incredibly strong. You can really put your body into scraping. This feels good and gets the job done. The only places you need to be a bit gentler around are the holes and knife marks. They have already been weakened and are more apt to tear. Flesh all surfaces right to the edge but ignore tiny bits of this and that, clinging to

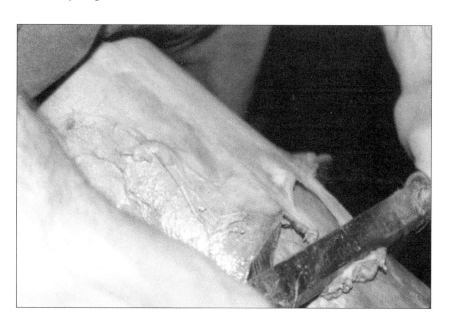

To scrape flesh off the edge of the hide, simply continue your stroke off of the hide and onto the beam. You will occasionally scrape off some of the wood, but this is not a problem.

Bucking

In this step you will make an alkaline solution to soak your hide in out of wood-ashes, hydrated lime or potassium hydroxide (the active ingredient in wood-ashes). The alkalinity will clean the protective mucus out of the hide interior so that the oils can thoroughly penetrate the hide. It will also swell the grain layer and make it much easier to see and remove. Doing this step correctly will make your hide scrape well and soften the first time through.

Making The Solution

There are separate directions for making the solution out of softwood ash, hardwood ash or hydrated lime. Hardwood and softwood ashes contain significantly different concentrations of alkali and thus need to be treated differently from one another. Many woods do not fall into such neat and tidy categories. Is alder a hard wood or soft wood? How about cottonwood? Perhaps you are burning many types of wood in your fire. What then? To deal with these vagaries, simply choose whichever category (hardwood or softwood) best describes what you are working with. Follow the directions and adjust as necessary. If really in doubt you can strain the solution out of the ashes through a burlap sack or hopper and use the egg test that is described under hardwood ashes.

Using Potassium Hydroxide

For one to two hides, put ten gallons of water in a plastic or wooden barrel (30 gallon plastic trash cans work fine). Add 4 oz. of KOH

(potassium hydroxide) or Red Devil Lye (sodium hydroxide) to the water and stir. IMPORTANT: Always add lye to water, not water to lye. To soak several hides, put 8 oz. in 20 gallons of water. Simple as that.

Using Hydrated Lime

Mix two lbs. (a half gallon) of lime with ten gallons of water. It's impossible to make it too strong because the lime reaches saturation in water at a good concentration (any extra precipitates to the bottom of the barrel). There should always be enough lime that some of it does settle out. This is the extra that can be stirred up each time the solution is used, to bring it back up to full strength. Use more than you need.

Using Soft-Wood Ashes

There is no risk of making a softwood ash solution too strong so the egg test (see hardwood ashes, later) is unnecessary. It should be about as thick as a milk shake (If you forget what this is like you may need to go out and get yourself one). Start with at least three gallons of ash per hide. More is better. Then slowly add water to the rest of the ashes, stirring as it is added. You are trying to get all of the ash wet, but not watery, so take your time. Once all of the ash is wetted it is time to find that milk shake consistency. If the solution is dry like dough add water. If it is runny enough that upon settling there is a large pool of water on top, then it is too wet. Add some ashes.

It is important to get the consistency right. If it is runny, it'll be weak and not very effective. If it is too dry, there isn't enough moisture to transport the alkali to the hide surface, and in.

A note: My experience with softwood ashes is very limited. This recipe has worked quite well though, and tests indicate that any weaker would just be too weak. Use something else if possible.

Tip: Always save out some extra ashes so that you can increase the strength of your solutions when necessary.

Using Hard-Wood Ashes

The trick with hard wood ashes is to make the solution strong enough but not too strong. There is a specific gravity test that was popular with pioneers, and it works really well. They would use a chicken egg to measure the strength. For comments on why pH paper is not as accurate, see *Tanning Reference* p. 143.

1. Using a wooden or plastic container, mix two parts (at least two gallons, preferably more) white wood-ash with one part water.

2. Let settle for fifteen minutes or more. If the ash is still suspended in the solution you will get a false reading. Remove excess charcoal.

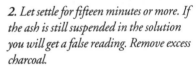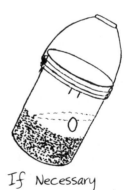

No   If Necessary

3. Place an egg in the solution. Make sure that the egg has enough space to sink or float, rather than just sitting on the layer of ash. If it doesn't, you may need to tilt the bucket in order to perform the following test.

B
U
C
K

4. The Incredible Floating Egg Test

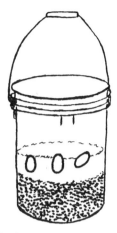

If the egg sinks or just barely floats, the solution is too weak. Add ash, allow to settle for ten min. and retest

If the egg floats and turns sideways, then the solution is too strong. Add a little water, stir, allow to settle for 10 min. Retest.

If it floats so that an area the circumference of a quarter to a half dollar is exposed, it is perfect.

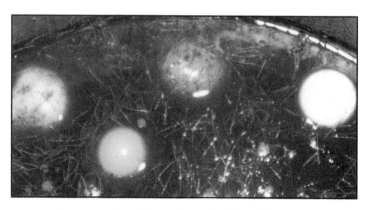

These eggs and spuds show what it should look like

5. When perfect, re-stir so that the ash and water are totally mixed. This makes it easier to get the hide in, and coated with the solution.

When The Solution Is Made

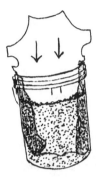 

Place hide(s) in solution; slosh around, until all surfaces are coated. Inspect the hide to make sure of this. The minimum amount of solution you need is enough to coat the hide completely. I like to use more.

Weight so that no hide sticks above surface. Then cover with a tight lid. These alkaline soaks are strong enough that you don't want your children to fall in them or your dogs to drink from them.

After every contact with alkali, rinse your hands until they no longer feel slippery. Alkali can dry your skin out like a harsh soap. It also helps to rub in some moisturizing oils. Another option is to wear rubber gloves.

How Long to Soak the Hide

It is hard to pin down exactly how long a hide needs to soak. While there are definitely some visual and tactile indicators, there are some typical times:

	Thin hide	Thick hide
Cold Weather	3+ days	4+ days
Hot Weather	2+ days	3+ days

The other two indicators are the swollenness of the hide and how easily the hair falls out. If the hide seems noticeably swollen, clip off a little piece of hide from the neck (the thickest part of the hide). An unswollen hide will appear bluish-white and floppy, while a swollen hide will be a brownish-yellow (tawny), thick and less stretchy. Sometimes you can even see that the flesh side of the hide will be swollen while the hair side is still bluish. I recommend relying on time, as it is the easiest to judge, and then using swollenness as a backup. If you start graining and notice that part of the hide is not swollen, put it back in the buck or you will have problems softening. For further discussion see p. 143.

Once the necessary amount of time has passed, it is at your convenience to scrape whenever you want within the following week. It will not hurt your hide to over soak it. The alkali create a near sterile environment: preventing bacterial buildup, rot, and rank smells. Soak longer than ten days and you are beginning to push your luck. In really hot weather I would limit this to six days.

If you follow the directions, this step is simple to do correctly. It is very important, as it makes all of the following steps easier.

When bucking is complete

Hand wring the hide as you remove it from the solution. The wood ash juice can be reused on other hides, with no loss of strength. Lime juice should only be reused twice and then disposed. It will get too weak. If the hide has been soaked in wood ashes you should make a concerted effort to rinse the ashes off of the surface. This can take a considerable amount of water. A good strategy is to put the hide in a big tub of water and slosh it around with the water running, or to lay it out on the ground and hose it down. Try to work the ashes out of the hair side. If you don't clean the ashes off well, the hide will get stained.

Graining

Be certain your scraper has the correct edge before starting (see p. 56).

Removing the grain is the hardest step to learn from a book. Knowing how deep to scrape is crucial to learn and is a very tactile experience. The most common mistake is to remove the hair and epidermis, but leave the grain. The grain is a distinct layer with some thickness to it, while the epidermis is just a thin to almost nonexistent layer. Just remember that if your tool isn't sharp, you can't scrape *too* deep. Follow directions carefully and you will be sure to get it all, from the beginning. Then, methodically scrape the rest of the hide. It might feel like work.

Getting Started

Lay the hide on the beam with the neck uppermost and the flow of hair running away from you. Lean, pinching several inches of over-hanging neck between your abdomen and the beam. Use your scraper to remove the hair from a two inch by two inch area. Now scrape that same patch as hard and deep as you can to remove the grain. Scrape by pushing the tool down into the hide, and then forward, in one continuous motion. It is a smooth motion, but with bite and force. If your tool is just running over the grain, make your motion shorter and choppier. Be aggressive! You're not going to hurt the hide, especially not on the neck, not even if you try your hardest.

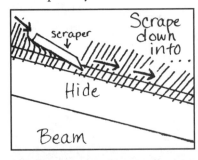

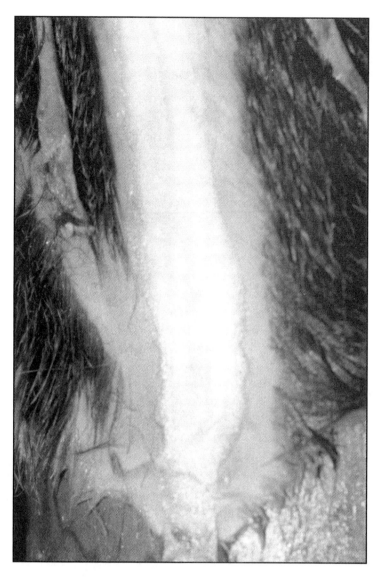

The lighter strip down the middle has had the grain removed. Some of it hangs off at the bottom. There is a solid layer of grain in between the scraped area and the hair to the right. The grain is darker and if you look closely you can see that it is distinctly raised relative to the area that has been scraped. Scrape this first section as deeply as you can. If you are not getting anything solid off an area, you either are not scraping hard enough, or something needs to be adjusted in your set-up (see Guide To Easier Scraping p. 145).

Scraping Basics

Teach Yourself to Scrape Efficiently

From the patch that you have started, scrape into bordering sections of grain like a snow plow, pushing it in front of the tool. Always work from a scraped section into an unscraped one.

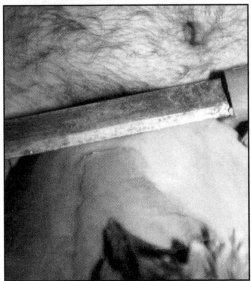

Your scraper should contact the hide well before the grain you intend to remove.....

...so that you can plow into it. Continue your stroke forward as far as you can maintain full pressure, then come to a complete stop!

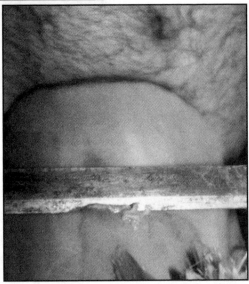

Your scraper will remove grain in strips. Take overlapping strokes so that there are no little strips left in between. Often your stroke will remove the bulk of grain from a strip but will leave some remnants. This is particularly common with young deer. By **repeating and overlapping your strokes**, you will be more likely to remove all of the grain.

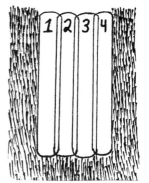

Overlap Strokes

When you are done with the first section, readjust the hide and scrape from the grained section into an adjacent unscraped section. When this new section is completely scraped, work from there into another adjoining patch, and so on....

Always completely scrape the section of hide that is right in front of you. Be certain that you've gotten all of the grain. Here is a good way to make sure:

Let the hide show you if you've got it all

To be sure that you have removed all of the grain, scrape the spot *really* intensely. With the exception of thin areas or obvious weak spots, this means as hard as you can. If you remove some really solid stuff, small sheets, you know that you were missing grain. If you only get miniscule amounts of hide crud, you already got it all.

The hide will let you remove all of the grain but no more. This is because you are separating layers rather than cutting into them (as long as your tool isn't too sharp).

There is certainly no need to 'scrape as hard as you can' all of the time, but you do want to scrape a little harder than you need to. Periodically 'scraping as hard as you can' will show you whether or not you are generally getting it all, or if you need to be more aggressive. With experience you'll get a feel for scraping, and intuitively know when you've gotten it all. It will be built into your rhythm. But whenever you are in doubt you can use this test. Let the skin teach you how to scrape!

G
R
A
I
N

Do not scrape new areas until you've completely removed the grain from where your are! If you methodically and thoroughly remove all of the grain from one spot before moving on, the neighboring sections of grain will remain distinct and raised. If you repeatedly scrape over the grain without fully removing it and keep moving around to taste test different little spots, then you compress and squeeze the water from the grain, making it nearly indistinct from well scraped sections. You won't be able to see what's done and what isn't. You will then become confused, disheartened and suicidal. **Avoid this at all costs!** This is the most common mistake beginners make. It is the most important skill to learn to scrape efficiently and enjoyably.

Now that we're done with the heavy handed advice, and you've got that methodical approach built into your style, it's time to let loose and scrape away.....

A Few Good Things To Keep In Mind When Graining....

*   Your hide should look and feel swollen from the alkali. If it isn't, the grain will be much harder to see and remove, and you will need to do the dressing step more than once to get the hide ready to soften. Sometimes if the solution was too weak, the thinner areas of the hide will be nicely swollen but the backbone and neck won't be. Areas that aren't swollen will have a whitish-blue coloring, rather than yellow-brown. Unswollen areas also have more stretch to them. If this is the case, you need to readjust your solution to the right strength, and put your hide back in it for a few days. It will make a big difference.

*   Continually readjust your hide, so that what you are working on is in the optimum position for comfort and effectiveness.

*   Try to scrape in the general direction that the hair flows, or sideways to it. When you scrape against it, you cut off the hair roots, leaving them in your hide.

*   Don't waste time pushing hair off without removing grain. Hair can be a helpful indicator as to what you have and have not scraped.

*   If it's a hot day and your hide is drying out quickly, have a bucket of water handy to soak the hide in from time to time.

....And Some Textures You May Wonder About:

* little white lines made by your tool. These are just temporary tool marks, caused by the displacement of moisture.

* larger white lines that are permanently on the hide. These are scars from the animal's life. Some hides have a lot. Some have none. They are especially common on the backbone. You can not scrape them out, but you should scrape them extra well to get all of the grain.

* grain that sinks into the hide and can't be removed. There is probably a deep knife cut on the other side. Flip the hide over to see if this is the case. If the skin is pretty thick you can often finesse the grain out by scraping from different angles. If it is pretty thin, just let it be. It's better to have a bit of grain than a big old hole.

Graining the rest of the hide

Once you've gotten a good start, there are two possible strategies. You can either scrape the neck, which is the hardest section to do, and get it over with while you are still fresh. Or you can scrape the rest of the hide, get into a really good scraping rhythm and then come back to the neck. In what ever order you choose to do these, here are some idiosyncracies of scraping necks, edges and holes:

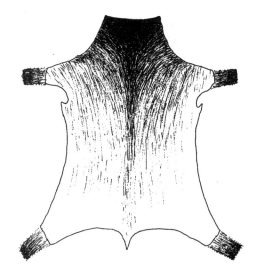

Dark shading indicates relative difficulty of scraping. The outer regions of the legs are hard to scrape and easily torn, a bad combination. Most people cut them off. Notice that where you started scraping was one of the hardest sections of the hide.

On *the neck* the grain grips the fiber core tightly. It pays to take shorter choppier strokes that concentrate your force into a smaller area. Don't be afraid to just wail on it with all of your drive and force. If the neck is really hard to scrape you can use a narrower beam. This will also concentrate your force into a smaller strip, making it much easier to remove (see neck beams p. 59).

Some necks are fairly easy to scrape, just a bit harder than the rest of the hide. If this is the case, scrape it and give thanks.

Scrape up the center of the neck, and then scrape sideways. This minimizes the amount of hair roots (black specs) that you leave in the hide.

As you get closer to *the edges* there is some chance of tearing the hide. It really varies. I wouldn't worry about it at all on a thick hide, while it is a good idea to lighten up the pressure a bit on thin ones. Fortunately the grain also comes off easier in these areas. Be sure to remove all of it.

Darker shading indicates the thinner, weaker skin of the deer's arm pits and groin.

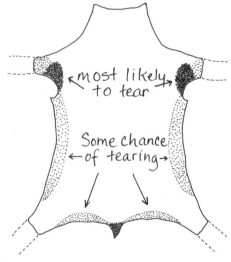

When you scrape an *edge*, position the edge so that it is pinned close to your waist. This way, the edge is held in place firmly, rather than squirming around. To scrape, simply continue your stroke right off the edge and onto the beam. You will occasionally remove a little wood, but this will not harm the beam. Scrape directly over the edge rather than trying to follow the flow of hair.

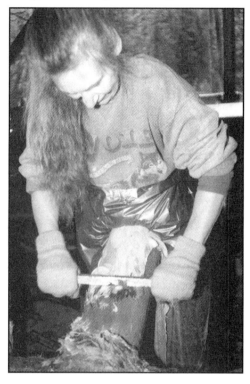

Our friend Ann used to be an astronaut. Now she wears the trunks of her spacesuit to scrape hides. Whatever works...

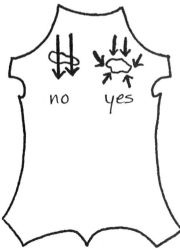

Bullet *holes* are quite strong and you will rarely aggravate them. Holes created by skinning, weak scar tissue and any other tears need special treatment.

Instead of scraping across these holes, scrape toward them from various directions. It's better to scrape against the hair than to make the hole bigger.

What Happens If You Don't Get it All?

It will be harder for the brains to penetrate and soften the hide. If you leave a strip of grain, it will usually come out stiffer. If you just leave some remnant of the *lowest* levels of grain, it will soften. However, when your hide is smoked, the smoke will not color any grain, or grain remnants. They will show up as white streaks, showing you what you have missed. These can be very pleasing and beautiful, just adding to the uniqueness of the hide. Accept and enjoy those white streaks when they happen, but to insure softness try to remove all of the grain. This is one of the most important steps in the process to learn to do well.

Plan on spending three or four hours graining your first hide, though it may take more or less time. It's more important to do a good job and enjoy the process. With experience, removing the grain becomes faster and easier. Your strokes become more effective. You spend less time wondering if you got it all. You develop a working rhythm. You start singing your favorite songs.

The Value of Video or Hands-on Instruction

Graining is one of the hardest steps to show you in a book. If you can get some hands-on instruction or watch the *Deerskins into Buckskins Video* (see p. 238), it'll really help you to understand what you are doing.

Rinsing

You need to get all of the alkalinity and swelling out of the hide. This can be done in moving water, or in a bucket with weak acids. For either method, you usually just need to stick the scraped hide in its place and leave it over night. However, hides and conditions can vary considerably, so it is important that you understand what is happening and use your senses to decide when rinsing is complete, rather than relying blindly on any 'recipe'. This is a very simple process.

How to:

In Moving or Voluminous Water

This can be a creek, river, lake or a hose in a tub. I highly recommend rinsing in naturally moving water, even if it is half a mile away. It is the easiest way to do this. You can put the hide under a couple of rocks, tie it to a rope or let it settle to the bottom of a pool (dehaired hides sink). Overnight is almost always long enough, except with thick hides in slow moving snow melt. The warmer the water, the faster the hide will rinse. In moving sixty degree water it should only take a few hours.

A Bucket With Weak Acids

Put three gallons of warm water and a pint of cider vinegar in a five gallon bucket. Put the hide in and slosh around occasionally. Do not use more than a pint of vinegar as you don't want to turn the hide acid, just bring it to neutral. If after 12 hrs. it is still swollen, make a new solution with a cup of vinegar to three gallons of water. This recipe is for a 'medium' sized hide. If your hide is small and thin, start with only a cup of vinegar.

Rinsing is Complete When...

...the hide has lost all signs of swelling. A good thing to do is to look at the hide part way through the process. At this point the thin edges of the hide will have returned to their soft and bluish-white state, while the thicker neck and rumps will still be swollen and tawny hued. This is a really graphic way to show yourself the difference. Rinsing is complete when all sections of the hide have returned to soft and supple land.

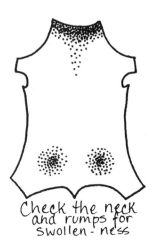

Check the neck and rumps for Swollen-ness

When in Doubt

Sometimes in really cold water, the hide will have rinsed but feel a bit tight. If you pull on it, it should loosen up, if it doesn't it needs to rinse more. There is a point when the whole hide will look like its soft but parts will still *feel* a bit swollen. At this point everything will have rinsed out except the interior of the thick sections. The neck will be the last part to fully release its alkalinity. *If in doubt,* check there. You can even clip off a small piece from the neck and look at the layers of the skin. If the interior looks swollen and tawny, it needs to rinse more. If it's in a bucket, put in a fresh solution.

It won't hurt the hide to leave it in the rinse longer than necessary. Bacteriologically, it is at ground zero, and it will take quite some time for bacteria to move in. I typically throw mine in the creek over night and take them out some time the next day (or two) depending on when I get around to it.

If you dress a hide that is still partly swollen you will not get all of the benefits of the bucking process. The swollen areas will come out stiff and need to be redressed!

How Rinsing Works

Mucus removal is a cleansing process. Part of that process is to thoroughly rinse the mucus and alkalinity out of the hide. This takes some time because hides are very tightly woven. Alkalis seek balance with any solution they are in. If you put a hide in a tub of plain water, the alkalis will leave the hide and enter the water, until the water and the moisture in the hide are of the same alkalinity. In a five gallon bucket, the hide and water will reach their equilibrium at a point that is still much too alkaline. So you have to change the water as many as eight to ten times over the course of one to two days. This is the hard way to go about rinsing. In moving water, that alkalinity gets whisked away by the current, so the hide will release all of its alkalinity, and do it faster, until it is the same p.h. as the creek. Unless you are rinsing an industrial quantity of hides, the creek is tiny or it soon empties into a small pond; it will not adversely affect the creek. The amount of alkalinity is small, and the dilution factor large.

If you don't have access to abundant moving water you should think about moving. Until then you can use weak acids in a bucket of water to rinse and neutralize the hide. As the alkalinity leaves the hide, it combines with the acids to form water and mineral salts. As long as there is still some acidity in the water, the alkali will continue to exit the skin.

R
I
N
S
E

Acidifying

(Optional, but recommended)

I f you choose not to do this step, then proceed straight to membraning. If you do choose to do this step, it will change how you do the wringing and braining steps. I recommend this step, it was the main impetus for this second edition, and here's why:

Brain tanned hides are known for their softness, but once in a while a hide comes out so incredibly soft that you have to wonder "how do I get all of my hides to turn out like that!". The trick is to get the hide slightly acidic before dressing it. It takes about 15 minutes of effort, and has a slew of benefits:

* Hides can be dressed while totally dry, giving them predictable, uniform brain penetration and removing the very variable process of getting the perfect moisture content.

* You don't have to wring the hide before braining it.

* Hides are easier to soften.

* Hides come out extremely soft.

Make the Solution (choose one)

In a Weak Vinegar Bath

After completing the 'Rinsing' step, put your hide (or two) in a five gallon bucket, with 4 gallons of warm bath temperature water and a 1/2 cup of vinegar. Leave it for 15 minutes while stirring a few times. Do not leave it for much longer than 15 minutes (30 max) or it can get too acidic. The hide will start to swell just like when it was bucked.

A little bit of swelling is normal and okay, but you don't want it to swell all over or get thick and rubbery. If it does, rinse as in the *Rinsing* chapter.

In Fertilizer (Ammonium Sulphate) Water

Put one cup (10 oz.) of ammonium sulphate (a common fertilizer, though be sure to use a pure form with no additives) into 20 gallons of warm bath temperature water. Stir. Add up to four hides. Leave it overnight, stirring at least three different times. That's it, or combine this with the 15 min. vinegar bath for even better results.

In Manure or Sour Brains

You could also use what some American Indian tribes used. Take a couple shovel fulls of buffalo dung and mix with four gallons of warm bath temperature water, or take a bucket of sour brain soup (must smell sour not putrid), put one or two hides in it overnight, and stir occasionally. References to native tanners using buffalo dung or sour brains are actually quite frequent in old accounts, though I haven't found a way to prevent the dung water from staining the hide.

These materials are rather variable, so a ph meter is very handy until you have some experience with how it should look and feel. You need a meter that measures ph to the tenth (ie. 6.1, 6.2, 6.3), and if you plan on using one regularly, get one that is waterproof. A ph of 5.8 to 6.4 is ideal, with the lower range giving you particularly soft hides.

Changes
Flesh
Buck
Grain
Rinse
+ Acidify
Membrane
+ Dry
~~Brain~~
~~Wring~~
Brain
Wring
Soften
Smoke

How to Proceed

* Membrane as described in next chapter.

* Then, allow hide to dry completely, or at least until the entire hide is on the dry side of 'the perfect moisture content'(see description on p. 99). No need to wring.

* Then, prepare the dressing (see p. 100). Put the dry hide into the solution. Crunch the hide down so that it is completely submerged. You can really force it in there as it won't tear. Let it soak for at least 20 minutes (longer is better,overnight being ideal, because the hide will relax and you'll go to less effort getting the hide totally soaked up).

* Then proceed from "Soak Your Hide" at the bottom of p. 100 and continue on with *The Basic Method*. I normally skip the second braining recommended there, but if its your very first hide, you should do it for insurance purposes.

Simple Acids vs Acid Salts

Your goal is to lower the ph of the hide to around 6.0 (7.0 is neutral, so this is slightly acidic) before braining it. Acids come in two forms: simple acids such as vinegar, and acidic salts, such as those contained in manure, or ammonium sulphate.

When you place a hide in a simple acid solution, the hide will absorb the acidity until the hide and the water are the same ph. Depending on the how much vinegar is used, the size and thickness of the hide, and how alkaline it is, they could reach equilibrium at a ph of anywhere from 4.0 to 10.0. By using a tried and true recipe, the variability greatly décreases, but there will always be some because every hide is of a different thickness and size.

Acidic salts, on the other hand, will continually release acid until the solution is the same ph as the salt (or until the acidic salt is all used up). The advantage of acidic salts is that they will lower the ph to a specific level but no more. There's no danger of going too far or of using too much, though you can use too little. Animal manures usually contain acidic salts which is one reason they were historically used by tanners (they also have beneficial enzymes). Ammonium Sulphate is a common fertilizer that is an acidic salt that drops the ph to just about the right level.

Membraning

Take your hide and re-scrape the flesh side of the hide, removing and breaking up the membrane layer. The membrane is a layer of loose fibrous tissue that doesn't have a clear end. If any solid patches of membrane are left on the hide it will make softening more difficult, and inhibit smoke penetration. So be systematic, scraping every inch, but don't worry about removing every last bit of membrane, it's not *that* important.

Use the same strokes and techniques that you grained and fleshed with. If the hide has dried out, a short soak in water will make membraning easier. Be extra conscious not to scrape over folds and ripples as they may cut.

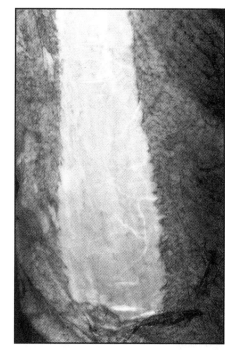

The clean strip down the center has been membraned, while the rest hasn't. The membrane on this hide was stained by the wood ashes. It really shows the texture of loose fibers well. The membrane on unstained hides is not nearly this obvious, frequently being the same color as the rest of the hide. In this case you should rely on systematic scraping rather than visuals.

This is the same stained hide. The solid black lines moving from the top left to the bottom right are knife cuts. Beginners are frequently frustrated trying to scrape off these marks, which isn't possible. The light white lines that are vertical in this picture are indentations created by the scraper. These indentations are normal and temporary, the result of extra water being squeezed out.

Congratulations! You've gotten your hide scraped and you're ready to work on getting it soft...

Wringing

Wringing removes all of the excess moisture from between the fibers of the hide, so that the dressing can enter and coat them. *The ideal is to have the fibers of your hide moist, but no water in between them, like a sponge ready to absorb.* When too much water is present, the dressing doesn't go there, because the space is already occupied. If the hide is too dry, the fibers have already glued themselves to each other. These glue bonds can be penetrated by water but not by the oils (hide glue and oil repel each other). After mucus removal, this is the key to great brain penetration. If the mucus is fully removed, and your hide basically damp, your hide will come out soft. Your efforts with getting the moisture content just right will determine just how uniformly soft it is.

How to:

To wring you need a horizontal bar, two or three inches in diameter, that won't break. This could be a pole that you have tied or nailed in place, or just the branch of a tree. Whatever you use, it should be smooth for at least a one foot section so that the hide is not punctured. Likewise, the hide should be free of sand or other debris that can create small holes.

Tip: On cold days soak your hide in really warm water before wringing. This will keep your fingers from feeling like they're going to fall off.

step 1: *Hang the hide over the bar. Use your hands to twist the hide and wring out excess water.*

step 2: *Hang the hide on the backside of the bar, so that the tail end of the deer is on the bar and the neck hangs down. You want the tail end to hang over for about six inches.*

**W
R
I
N
G**

step 3: *Bring the neck up over the tail end, from the front, so that it overlaps the tail and hangs down the backside for a few inches. It now looks like a big hide loop.*

step 4: *Starting at one side, roll the edges of the hide toward the center of the loop. Make sure that the whole side is rolling in evenly and tuck in any flaps of skin as you go.*

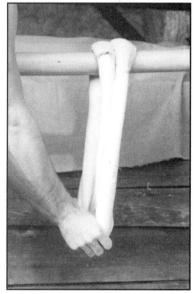

Then roll the other side in until they meet in the middle.

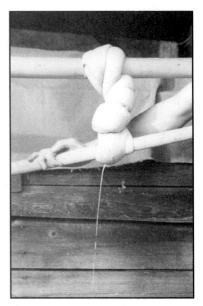

W
R
I
N
G

step 5: *Place a smooth, strong stick of axe handle size through this hide loop and twist to one side.*

Continue twisting until you can twist no more. You can put a lot of force into it. Medium to thick hides should be twisted as hard as you can. *Thin hides should not be torqued quite as hard. Allow liquid to stream out until it is just a drip.*

step 6: Untwist, and repeat in the opposite direction. The next time you untwist the hide, rotate the hide loop a quarter turn. Twist in both directions. **Continue until you have twisted eight times in four positions.** If available, use a towel or rag to absorb any extra surface moisture, when the hide is fully twisted the last two times.

step 7: When wringing is complete, undo the hide. There should be few soggy spots. If there are a lot of soggy areas, you need to roll it back up and wring again. This time with a little more force.

When you feel the hide has been wrung as well as possible, un-roll and stretch it wide open. This will take a few minutes. A lot of what you stretch should turn white. Try to get rid of the bulk of the ripples.

Use the edge of your scraping beam, as well as your hands to stretch the hide open after wringing.

step 8: Once the hide is well stretched open, it is time to assess the moisture content. One indicator of wetness is color. Blue spots are too wet. Gray areas are marginally too wet. Tawny areas are dry enough, and white sections are tawny areas that have been stretched open. Tawny and white are ideal. Gray areas are good enough. Blue areas are generally too wet. Another good test is to run your finger along the underside of the hide and push moisture out the top side. If you can push water out, then that spot is too wet. Use your beam and scraper tool to squeegee moisture out of any wet spots. You can push the moisture toward the edges and off, or redistribute it to a really dry area.

The thoroughness and quality with which you perform this step will greatly influence how soft your hide is, and how easily it softens! Remember, wherever there is loose water the dressing can not go, frequently resulting in a stiff spot.

When you are done wringing, soak the hide in the dressing. Don't let it dry out in the mean time. If you need to do something first, roll the hide up tightly and put it in a plastic bag.

Dressing

Prepare a Dressing

Brains. For each hide, take anywhere from half a pound to a full pound of fresh or thawed out brains and mix with a cup of hot water. Then use your fingers to mash and mutilate the brains into a paste, or stick them in a blender on liquefy. The goal is to make your solution soupy, not lumpy.

Eggs. Beat one dozen eggs.

Soap and Oil. Grate a 1/4 bar of soap. Add a 1/4 cup of neat's foot oil.

Then in a two to five gallon container, mix the dressing with a half gallon of bath temperature water. I like what I can barely stand to hold my hand in. The heat will help the solution soak in faster and with less effort from you. *If it's too hot for you, it's too hot for the deer's skin.*

Soak the Hide

Put the well wrung hide (or dried if you 'acidified' it) in and slosh it around until it is completely coated by the dressing. The dressing needs to soak into every pore and fiber of the skin. The hide will feel soft and loose where it has soaked up enough. Any spots that did not get fully stretched open after wringing will need some stretching.

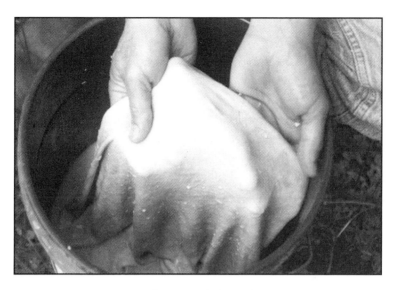

Massage and stretch the hide into the dressing

Give particular attention to the edges of the hide and holes. If they are not fully soaked up, use your fingers to pull them out.

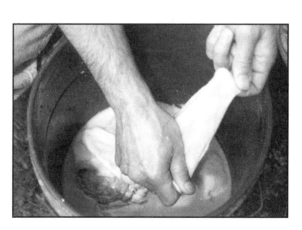

Stretch the edges by pulling your thumb and fore finger toward the edge and off.

Put a tight lid on the bucket as the hide soaks. Otherwise, many bugs will come taste these oily treats, drown and lay there waiting to greet you upon your return.

D
R
E
S
S

The hide can soak for twenty minutes to overnight, depending on what is convenient for you. More time will make up for a lack of stretching and vice versa, though you may not need much of either. It is simply necessary that every spot on the hide gets completely saturated.

When you think your hide has completely soaked up the dressing, take it out and hang it over a pole, branch or any horizontal thing. Hang it so that the neck is hanging down. Your hide should be sloppy wet, everywhere. Pull from side to side, up and down the hide. With the exception of scar tissue, everything should stretch uniformly. If a spot puckers or resists stretching, use your fingers to pull it in several different directions, opening it up. Then put it back in the dressing for five minutes. If their are persistent ripples on the backbone even after re-soaking, then the bucking did not completely neutralize the mucus, or your hide was too dry when you dressed it.

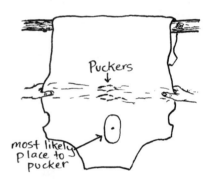

Look for tight puckers on the backbone when you stretch the hide width-wise.

Wring and Dress Your Hide Again

Wring your hide out again but catch your brain, egg, or soap solution in a bucket. Work the hide to the 'ideal moisture content' and soak it in the dressing one more time. If you do everything nearly perfectly, you can get away with wringing and dressing the hide only once. However, you will be much more likely to have your hide come out just right if you go back and do it all a second time. Over the years it has become very clear to me that those tanners who do dress a second time have more uniformly soft hides, and it beats going through the entire softening process only to find out that you need to re-dress anyway!

Storing Your Dressed Hide

(1) If you are ready to soften continue on.

(2) If not, you can refrigerate or freeze your hide until you are ready to wring and soften. Alternatively, you can wring the hide and then refrigerate or freeze it.

(3) Or you can dry your hide out and store it until you are ready to soften. To dry, lay it out in the sun. There should be no folds. Uncurl the edges. The more stretched open your hide is as it dries, the easier it will be to soak it up later, especially the neck. You can lay it on the grass, a bush, a log or whatever. You may want to be conscious of not getting dirt or anything that will stain on the hide. Sometimes trees will drip juices that will stain a hide. Pick a spot out in the open rather than under a tree. If it is raining, you will have to hang it inside. Prop the sagging areas open with some sticks so they don't shrink up too much. Dressed and dried hides can be stored indefinitely as long as they are protected from bugs, dogs and other critters.

Preparing To Soften

To get ready for softening you want to return your hide to the same condition it was in prior to dressing. The idea is to get rid of as much of the loose moisture in the hide as possible. It is only necessary to work the hide when it is transitioning from wet to dry. If you start softening a hide that is very wet in some spots, and just barely damp in others, then you are going to be softening a lot longer. You also have to focus more, because different sections are in different stages and need different things done to them.

If you dried your hide out after braining you will need to soak it for at least a few hours, and then wring it out. If your hide is wet and fresh out of the brains, its ready to wring. So do a thorough wringing job and then squeegee out any wet spots just like before, and proceed to softening.

Sewing Holes

Holes may be sewn after wringing but before you start softening. Sewing the holes at this point will allow the fibers to realign and dry flat around the closed hole. If you wait to sew until after softening it is harder to get the area around the hole flat. Well sewn holes can virtually "disappear" into the fiber fabric of finished buckskin. Sewing the holes will also prevent them from enlarging during the softening process, though this is an infrequent problem. If you are hand softening you can skip this step and simply patch the holes, when the hide is finished.

Tools

The best needles to use depends on how good a sew job you want versus what you are comfortable working with. You also need a sharp pair of scissors.

* *The best sew job, easy to push through but the needles are tiny* (and thus not for some folks): short #12 beading needles, beading thread or backstrap sinew. The small size of these needles allows them to slide between the fibers rather than trying to push them out of the way. This makes it easy to push them through and they leave very tiny holes.

* *The easiest but worst sew job*: small glover's needles with strong thread or backstrap sinew. Specially designed for leather working, these triangular needles cut their way through. They leave rather large holes in their wake. Get glover's needles at leather working shops or some fabric stores.

* *Good sew job but the hardest to push through*: small regular needles with strong thread or backstrap sinew. The thinner they are the easier they push through and the smaller hole they leave. These leave moderate sized holes.

Thin vs. Thick Needles

Thinner needles are easier to push through and leave smaller holes. They slide right through the fibers, rather than having to shove them aside. However, some folks just can't deal with threading and using really small needles. If you are one of them, use the smallest needle you are comfortable with.

The smaller the needle the smaller the thread needs to be and the closer the stitches should be taken. The need for more stitches is compensated for by the ease of stitching. Further, this type of stitching does not rip out as easily.

How to

You do not want your hide to dry too much while you are sewing. Set yourself up in the coolest spot available and keep the hide folded up. Decide which holes are worth sewing. I always sew all of the holes that are in the midst of the main body of the hide. I also sew weak spots that are on the verge of being holes. I do not sew holes that are right on the edges of the hide, or I do a quick and callous job. I would suggest sewing any that will be within something that you plan to make. Your sew job will endure a lot of stress during the softening process. Do as good a job as you can so that it does not rip out later.

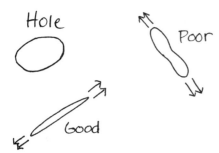

To start, make the hole sewable as a straight line. Even if a hole is round, you can stretch it and it will realign into nearly a straight line. Pull it in several directions to see which one provides the straightest line.

Fold the hole in half along this line, so that the flesh side is visible.

Usually it will create a "canoe" shape. Snip off the tips of the canoe, and any *stiff* or ragtag edges, so that the hole becomes as close to a straight line as possible, without making it huge. The straighter it is, the flatter it will lie after softening.

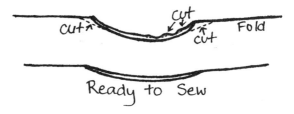

Cut a length of thread that is at least eight times as long as the hole. Thread it through the eye of the needle, make the two ends meet and tie them in an overhand knot. Make sure doubled over thread is not thicker than the hole that the needle makes or it will be a pain to pull through.

Don't push it from behind but from the sides

How to grip a beading needle

Starting at one end of the hole, push the needle through the buckskin and the loop at the back end of the thread.

Use the whip stitch, to sew the edges together. Keep your stitches close together, take an even bite of skin with each stitch, and pull them tight.

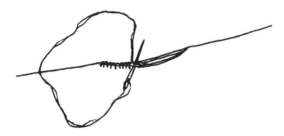

When you reach the end of the hole stick your needle into the hide as if you were taking another stitch, but only pull it part way through. Wrap the protruding needle three times with the thread that you left previously. Pull the needle all the way through and cinch. Repeat.

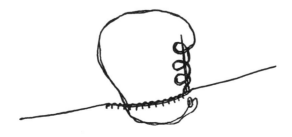

Softening

Softening is a very exciting part of the tanning process. This wet, sometimes unappealing mass of skin transforms into soft, luxurious buckskin! It is also the step that requires the most physical effort, and enough focus to stay with it to the end. Luckily the transformation is so cool that the energy needed is easy to come by.

You want to work in a warm environment, seventy to eighty degrees being ideal. Work outdoors in the sun or shade depending on how hot it is, or indoors in a heated space. Softening in a cool temperature takes forever. Softening your first hide in blazing hot weather can get very stressful and is bad for familial relationships.

Leave yourself a large open chunk of time with no other commitments other than softening the hide, and taking care of yourself. The amount of time it takes can vary wildly between one hour and six, depending on the temperature. It usually takes between two and four hours, but you should always leave the day open just in case. Softening is not something you can randomly leave to go answer the phone, or deal with the kids. You can take some short breaks but you need to go with the hide's timing, not your own. For this one chunk of time, the hide wishes to be your only focus. If you do have kids, a spouse or visiting friends, get them involved in the softening process with you. It's a lot of fun to stretch hides with others, and makes it that much less work.

There are two common methods: hand softening, and frame softening. While the techniques and tools vary somewhat, the same principles apply. They are both excellent methods. Frame softening requires some time to build a frame, to get your hide lashed into the frame and once you are in, you are pretty much committed until the end. However when the hide is in the frame, it is easier to work, can be enlarged and thinned, and the finished product will lay flatter for easy pattern cutting. Hand softening is easy to do almost anywhere: in the car, at the beach, by the woodstove. It also allows you to put the hide in a plastic bag to prevent further drying and finish it another day (this can only be done in the early stages). I use and enjoy both methods and their results. A more detailed comparison of the pros and cons of each method is offered in the *Tanning Reference* chapter on p. 155.

For now, we'll talk about some of the general principles involved so that you understand what you are doing. Then you can choose whether you want to hand soften or frame stretch.

There Are Two Objectives:

(1) **You must continually move, stretch and realign the fibers of the hide as it goes from *damp* to dry.** Hide fibers are composed partially of glues. These glues set up as your hide dries. When fibers are wet the glues will not set up. When they are lightly damp, the glues will start to set up. When dry, they will have locked neighboring fibers to one another, creating a solid sheet, with no give.

Your job is to move the fibers while they are setting up, so that they can not lock to one another. The interior fibers will go through this stage after the exterior fibers are mostly done. Because of this you will need to return to the same area and stretch it many times in order to prevent each layer from locking up. If you stop stretching your hide before the interior fibers are dry, they will lock up even though the exterior fibers dried soft and stretchy.

(2) **It is important to buff both the flesh and the grain sides of your hide, periodically as it dries.** If you do not buff the outer surfaces then a crust will form on them, preventing them from stretching fully. This will in turn inhibit the interior of your hide from stretching fully. Your hide will still soften, but it will not be nearly as loose and soft, and the surfaces will be a little crusty.

S
O
F
T
E
N

Get into it! Think of softening as an exercise workout. *Stretch, stretch,...rub, rub,... stretch this way, now that way...come on now, work out that stiffness.*

HAND SOFTENING

Tools

The best all around softening tool is a steel **cable**—for working edges, abrading surfaces and intensive stretching. While many other tools will do the job, the cable kicks butt. If you can get some **pumice**, it will give the surface an extra silky feel and help remove excess membrane. It is also really handy to have a way to hang the hide, either from a row of nails or ties. Cut five slits along the tail edge of your skin to hang it.

Getting Started

Unless it is very hot, your hide does not need to be worked really hard initially. This is a good time to get to know the hide and various stretching techniques.

1. Take your wrung and squeegeed hide and stretch it in various directions until all of the creases created by wringing are gone.

2. Stretch the skin by grabbing each side and pulling apart all the way up and down the hide. Next, stretch the hide from neck to tail. Then stretch the hide diagonally. Find various ways to pull and really stretch each small and large section of the skin in at least two directions. A pattern will help you go over all of the sections of the hide, each time around. This is the basic technique for stretching your hide. You will do this often as your hide dries.

> Do you like raw bleeding knuckles? If so, try to grab the hide with your knuckles curled in. Otherwise, make an effort to hold the hide between your thumb and *outstretched* fingers.

Hides can be stretched by pulling down over the knees, or simply by hand....

...between two or more friends...

...hanging from cords or nails...   *...or tossing friends in the air.*

SOFTEN

3. The thinner skin around the perimeter of the hide will dry first. These edges should be worked frequently until they are dry. Stretch the *edges* by pulling them out from the rest of the hide. Allow your thumb and finger to slide off the edge as you pull.

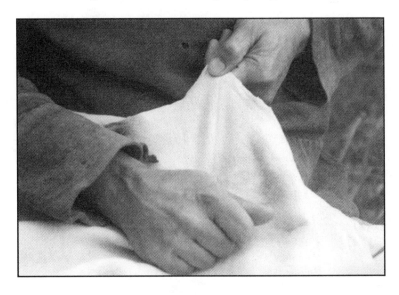

Edges can also be worked on the cable, by rapidly pulling the edge back and forth. The cable is especially effective on crusty edges that are hard for your fingers to pull open. It is good to use a combination of these two edge working techniques.

S
O
F
T
E
N

4. When a large portion of your hide has become white and stretchy, it is time to abrade the surfaces. Abrade an area until the crust is gone and the fibers appear buffed. Don't bother with areas that are still wet. Keep a balance between working each area effectively and covering the whole hide in a few minutes time.

The cable is wonderfully effective because it abrades the hide as well as stretches the fibers. It's important to concentrate the energy in one area at a time, so fold the hide over rather than bunching it up into a big wad. Then rapidly pull the hide back and forth over the edge. Readjust the hide in your hands to work the next strip. Try to avoid or at least go lightly over sewn holes, so that they don't tear. Using some kind of pattern will help you to give the hide a once over without having to think too much (Don't you get tired of thinking sometimes?).

Pumice and other hand held tools are easier to use if the hide is hung from thongs or a row of nails. Grip a piece of the hide to provide tension and aggressively rub back and forth.

S
O
F
T
E
N

Crunch Time

From the time that nearly all of the hide has become white and stretchy to the point that the edges are completely dry is the heart of softening. It is especially important to stay focused and exert yourself. Rotate between stretching the edges, the main body and abrading. Anytime a surface is less luscious than you wish it to be, abrade it! Otherwise, keep those fibers moving...

Use Your Senses

Softening is a very sensory skill. Your hide should feel like it is getting soft the entire time you work on it. If an area feels tight or stiff, work it concertedly. It should loosen up. Keep an eye out for places that don't give, don't move, with the rest of the hide. These areas will create puckers in the hide when you stretch them. This is the classic sign of an area that is stiffening up. Target these areas for extra attention. If they loosen up then it is a sign that they simply needed to be worked.

You can stop working an area when it feels soft, dry and it rebounds when stretched (rather than staying where you stretched it). If it is stretchy and soft but still *feels cool to the touch, or doesn't rebound, you need to keep working it.* Once an area is done rejoice! And then concentrate on the sections that are still drying.

Maintenance

When the edges of your hide are dry and it's down to the neck, butt cheeks and backbone, there are less areas to keep track of, so you can

S O F T E N

> **'Bagging It'**... If something comes up and you need to take a break, the hide can be rolled up tightly, with the wetter areas out, and placed in a plastic bag. Any extra air should be squeezed from the bag and the bag closed tightly. This will prevent further drying and redistribute some of the moisture. 'Bagging' should only be done when most of the hide is still damp, or else it may irreversibly stiffen.

take more short breaks and relax a bit. This is also the cutoff point for putting your hide into a plastic bag and finishing it later. At this point you are committed to the end. If you want to speed things up you can expose your hide to more heat (up to 120 degrees). The less areas that still need work the more heat you can keep up with.

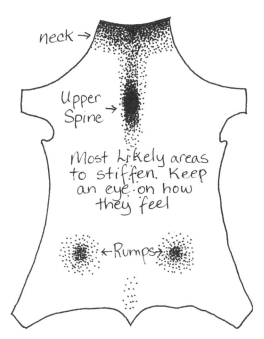

Check out this illustration of the common places that stiffen up on a hide. Keep a particular eye on these. Are they stretching like the rest of the hide? Or is there noticeably more resistance. If a spot feels tight and it is not one of these sections illustrated, it probably just needs some attention. Trust your senses. If it feels different, even when worked, then it is. If the dressing hasn't fully penetrated the hide, or section of the hide, it will not soften, no matter how hard you work it.

If a Section of the Hide Stiffens Up

If an area of the hide is feeling stiff, go to the cable or use your hands and wail on it in at least two different directions. If it won't relax and get stretchy, then it's not dressed well enough! Really wail on it to be sure. If it still feels like its stiffening, then it is... Redress it now! You may not want to but it *will* be worth it. If you wait, you won't get as good penetration, and you may end up redressing again and again. Roll the hide into a tight ball so that it doesn't dry any further while you are prepping the dressing. Wrap it in a plastic bag if one is available.

Another thing to remember about redressing is that the stretch-

S
O
F
T
E
N

ing work that you have put into your hide has changed things, and your hide will soften to the same point where you left off, very easily. Don't be afraid to redress. Your buckskin is going to last you a *very* long time, so you might as well have it come out as soft as you'd really like it to be.

Finishing

Keep working the hide until the neck and butt cheeks are dry and rebounding. They are the last places to dry, and the most likely to stiffen. If you quit before these are really done, they may stiffen up on you.

Sometimes softening can get to ya

S
O
F
T
E
N

FRAME SOFTENING

Necessary Tools

A **softening stick**. A straight, round, three foot long by two inch wide piece of wood (about ax handle size). Bevel one end. Make the beveled tip slightly rounded. It does not need to be sanded smooth, the hide will do that.

side view of tip

Six, twenty foot lengths of durable cordage. Use cordage that is about the size of clothes line cord or baling twine. Rope is thicker than necessary, while string is too weak. Have more on hand than you need.

Pumice. See p. 65.

A **frame** and be built out of poles or 2 x 4's.

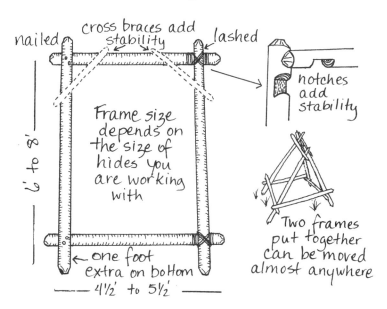

nailed

cross braces add stability

lashed

notches add stability

Frame size depends on the size of hides you are working with

6' to 8'

one foot extra on bottom

4½' to 5½'

Two frames put together can be moved almost anywhere

S
O
F
T
E
N

To Start

Work in a cool place until your hide is laced into the frame, so that it doesn't dry out prematurely. Then move it into the sun or other warm locale.

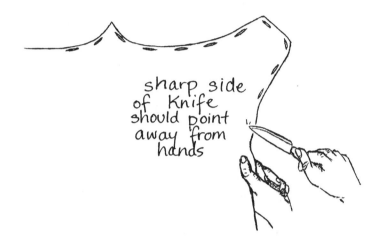

Take your wrung-out hide, a sharp tipped knife, and poke holes three to four inches apart all around the perimeter of the hide. Make these holes a 1/4 inch in from the edge and parallel to it. Having a piece of wood behind where you are poking makes this easier. Then, tie your hide into the frame in the following sequence:

SOFTEN

How To Hang The Hide For Frame Softening

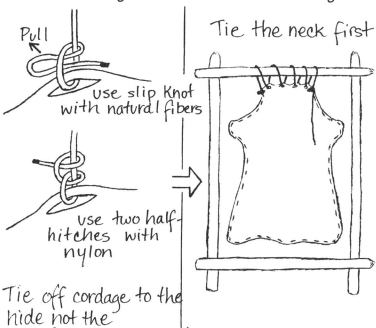

Pull

use slip knot with natural fibers

use two half-hitches with nylon

Tie the neck first

Tie off cordage to the hide not the
— frame —

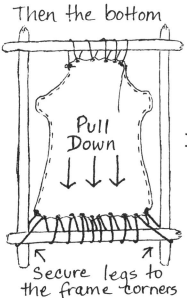

Then the bottom

Pull Down

Secure legs to the frame corners

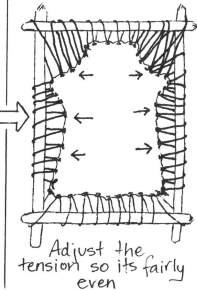

Then the sides

Adjust the tension so its fairly even

Basic frame softening techniques

Work your hide in a cool place using the following techniques, until you have a good grasp of what needs to happen. Then move the frame somewhere warmer.

Working the main body:
Use the wooden softening tool to *deeply* stretch the hide. You can really lean into it. Be a *little* more delicate around holes and obvious weak spots, such as knife marks from poorly skinned hides. Use a pattern to help you work every section regularly without having to think about it.

Lean into the hide and give it a nice deep massage. Hold one hand close to the front of the tool for leverage. Stroke it don't just poke it.

After working the hide for a while there will typically be too much slack on the sides and neck to effectively work the edges. Press a hand or knee into the hide to take up that slack, and stroke all the way to the edge.

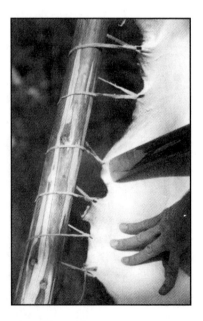

SOFTEN

The edges:
After the initial staking, go around the perimeter of the hide and *pull out the edges between thumb and forefinger. Allow the thumb and fingers to slide right off.* The edges will dry first, so give them regular attention from now until they are dry. You will always lose a thin perimeter to stiffness but doing this regularly will keep that to a minimum.

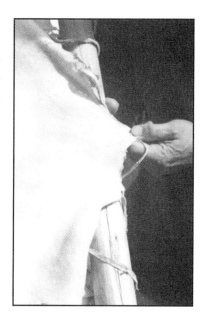

When you have gone over the whole hide once, notice which sections are farther along in the drying process than others. These are the areas to focus your energy on, while periodically working the entire hide. Ignore sloppily wet spots until they start to get drier. Remember, this should not be surface stroking, but deep tissue massage. If the hide gets so loose in the frame that it is sloppy and hard to work, tighten the cordage somewhat, leaving enough slack for the hide to stretch and rebound.

When most of the hide has whitened, **buff both sides with an abrading tool (like pumice).** This will get rid of the crust that will otherwise prevent the hide from stretching fully.

Finishing

From here on out you should follow the general instructions for hand softening starting with **"Crunch Time"**. Follow the same instructions but substitute the techniques and tools of frame softening. These are the key differences that you should keep in mind:

(1) The pucker test is not so effective on a frame though you can do it by pulling with your hands. Instead, you will feel the tool just slide over the tightening areas, rather than fully stretching the fibers. Give these areas extra attention. To assess whether these sections need

to be redressed, work them concertedly with your staking tool.

(2) You can stop working when an area feels totally dry, soft, and rebounds, rather than holds poke marks, you are done with this section. If it still feels cool to the touch then you need to keep working it.

S
O
F
T
E
N

Smoking Sacks

To get your hide(s) ready for smoking you glue, staple or sew them into a sack shape that is open on one end (the neck), similar to a pillow case. Then you sew a thick denim or canvas skirt onto the bottom of the sack. This will protect your buckskin from the heat of the fire and the dirt of the ground. Smoke will rise through this opening into the closed sack and have no where to go but into the hide. I like to glue my hide sacks together but most of my friends who have tried sewing machines prefer them. Some just use a regular needle and regular machine. A lot of folks also like to staple their hide sacks together. You need a fairly heavy duty stapler. You can also hand-sew but this takes longer, and makes the smoking take longer and be less even. Whether you choose to glue or sew your sack together follow these same general instructions.

Getting the Hides Ready

Frequently there will be an area from 1/8 inch to one inch around the perimeter of the hide that came out stiff. Trim this off, leaving only good soft buckskin. Then resew any holes that have ripped out, or any new ones that appeared during the softening. Always trim stiff edges from the holes before sewing. If you are planning to patch the holes after smoking you can temporarily stitch them up with 1/4 inch stitches or glue them shut.

I prefer to smoke hides in pairs. Hides smoked together usually come out the same color, which can be convenient for garments. The more similar your hides are in size and thickness, the better. If they are really different, it is better to smoke them separately.

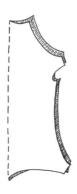 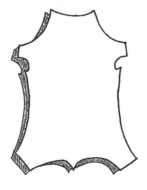

If you are smoking only one hide, fold it over on itself along the backbone, grain side in.

If you have two similar hides, lay them on a flat surface, one on top of the other with the grain sides facing in. Align the hides so that the necks line up, and the tail ends, and so on.

How to make the sack

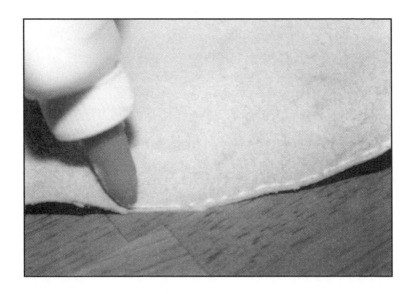

Starting at the tail, apply a **thin** *line of glue for one to two feet along the edge of one hide. Apply your line of glue about 1/8 inch wide, and don't worry about making it perfect.*

Gluing the Sack Together

Use Elmer's, hide or wood glue. Take a piece of paper and practice laying down the thinnest line of glue that you can. Adjust the cap so that less comes out at a time.

Then press the edges of your hides together along that glue line. Your glue should have gotten a bit tacky by the time you start to press the first edges together. Vary the length of each section of glue line to accommodate for how fast the glue is drying, (if fast, shorten length of section; if slow, lengthen it).

Follow the edges of your hide no matter how they are shaped. Just make everything meet and it will work. Thin protruding flaps of skin can be glued down to their own hide. Continue down one side until you start to turn the corner on the bottom of the neck. Then glue the other side (if you are doing two hides), until you reach the same spot. Don't drip glue on the hide, as it will interfere with smoke penetration, leaving a white spot on the hide.

Sewing the Sack Together

Start at the tail and sew down one side and then the other. If you are hand stitching use a glover's needle and take 1/4 to 1/2 inch stitches. Take several stitches before pulling the thread through. Use cheap thread so that it is easy to rip out later. Follow the crazy edges of the hide and just make them meet. Leave the neck open so that the finished sack is shaped like a pillow case.

The Goal

The tighter your sack seams the more smoke is trapped in the sack, rather than escaping through the seams. This allows pressure to build up and causes the smoke to penetrate the hide faster.

Glued seams are ideal for this. Sewing machine stitched seams are equally good. Hand stitched seams work too, but the tighter the better, and it's hard to get them as tight as glue!

S
A
C
K

How to make the skirt

Your skirt should be made from heavy cotton fabric. Denim works great. We use old blue jeans that we pick up at the thrift store. Don't use polyester or other synthetic fabrics. They catch fire too easily. The thicker and more tightly woven your skirt material, the less smoke will bleed through it, sending more smoke up into your hide sack.

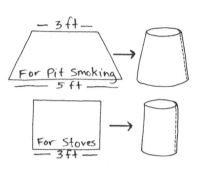

Sew the fabric into a cylinder on a sewing machine or by hand. It doesn't have to be perfect.

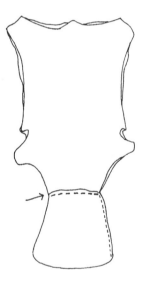

Joining Hide(s) and Skirt

Your hide(s) should now be glued or sewn into a pillow case shape. Next, using a glover's needle, sew the skirt onto the open end of the hide sack. Be sure to center it, so that it lays in line with the rest of the sack. Make your stitches about a half inch long. No need to be too finicky here, but the tighter the seam the less smoke you lose through it.

SACK

Smoking

Smoke permanently changes the nature of the hide fibers. It makes it so that the skin can be washed many times and dry as soft as the first time, with only a little help from you. It also colors the skin. The color gets darker the longer you smoke the hide. As the hide smokes it turns from white, to yellow, to brown; though it often has golden, bronze, orange, green, or gray highlights. The hide doesn't need to be smoked very long to be functionally tanned, so it is up to you how dark you'd like it to be.

Getting Ready To Smoke

Before starting the smoking process you will need a container within which to produce the smoke, a material that smokes a lot, and a way of hanging your hide over the smoker.

The Smoker

Choose one of the following three smoking contraptions. They all work, so it is mostly a matter of convenience. Choose a location for smoking that is well away from flammable materials, such as dry grass and leaves. If necessary, clear away anything flammable that is within three feet of your setup.

Dig a *pit* that is one and a half to two feet deep and narrower than the circumference of the opening of your hide sack (a foot across or more). You want this pit to have as much volume as is reasonably possible, but with a small enough opening for your hide sack to fit around. Dig the pit in an area that is easy to dig but of a sturdy soil. I prefer clay soils or anything that has a green grassy sod surface that will help prevent the top from caving in. This is the ideal, but you can get away with a lot.

Instead of a pit, you can simply use any appropriately shaped *metal or ceramic pot*. This pot should be at least a foot wide and a foot and a half deep. It should not have any holes in the side of it. You do not want a draft. A smudge pot is conveniently mobile, allowing you to move it out of the rain or to a different beautiful spot for smoking.

Small *wood stoves* that are fairly tight can be used for smoking. Old and drafty wood stoves should be avoided because they are harder to control and prone to flare-ups. It is preferable if the stove can be fed from the top.

Removable plates make it easier to add punk and monitor the heat

optional: extra length allows smoke to cool

Punk

For each hide collect at least half of a fifty pound grain sack of punky (rotten) wood. More is better. I use Douglas fir punk, but any will work. Avoid conifer pitch, which is concentrated around knots (where branches meet the trunk). Pitch is very flammable, the opposite of what you want. The punk should be obviously well-decayed, and easy to break in your hands. Collect punk that is chunky, between popcorn and small apple size. Avoid really fine stuff. You will naturally end up with some variation in size and this is good. Some materials that I have used that reliably give pleasant hues of yellow, brown, golden or bronze, are: Douglas fir, pine, alder, and cottonwood. Some folks use sagebrush or cedar to give their hides an aroma that they particularly like. I haven't heard of anybody smoking with materials that just didn't work, turned their hide electric pink, or smelled real bad. You might not want to use poison oak though....

For use, your punk should be dry or slightly damp. Damp or wet materials snuff out the fire too much. If the punk that you collect is wet, put some effort into drying it out. Otherwise smoking will be hellaciously slow.

The Hide Hanger

You want some contraption to hang your hide sack from, over the smoking pit. You need to be able to hang the sack from two points. We use a two tripod and cross beam system. You can also use a single tripod if its big enough, or the limb of a tree (adjusting the hanging height by adjusting the length of the thongs) (see smoking setup illus., p. 131). You need two to four thongs to suspend the hide from the hanger. We use buckskin scraps. You can use any cordage.

The Smoking Process

Once you have your smoker, punk and a way to hang the hide, you are ready to start smoking. It is always worth it to wait for good weather conditions. Smoke your hide(s) on still days with little to no chance of precipitation. Any serious breeze will make smoking a total hassle or impossible. You can get away with smoking in a very mild breeze but it can be challenging. Mornings are often the least breezy time of day and a good time to smoke.

You should take care of any and all bodily needs before you start smoking. Eat, go to the bathroom, have water on hand. Smoking can take anywhere from half an hour to two and a half hours, so

SMOKE

really set yourself up to be comfortable. While your hide is smoking, you need to pay attention to it! If a fire erupts in the smoking pit, and you are not present to smother it, your hide can burn into uselessness in the matter of a minute. Do not even be distracted by conversations ten feet away from your hide. You need to be right there. If you are present, you will have plenty of time to prevent a catastrophe.

I'm going to describe the smoking process using a pit smoker, because this is what I've been using lately. Using a pot is essentially the same, and a stove very similar.

Starting The Fire

To get things rolling you will need to create a solid bed of hot coals in the bottom of the pit. Hardwood coals are preferable. Create a good solid stick fire. When the fire has burned down to the point that it is just turning into coals, is the time to start. At this point there is still some flame, but the fire has predominantly turned to coals. It is very important to create a good bed of coals and to utilize them while they are in their prime.

Preparing The Sack

Use a knife or an awl to poke a hole in the upper corners of your hide sack Position the holes at a high point, an inch or two from the extreme outer edge. This will help the hide hang with no need for spread sticks on the inside.

Positioning the Hide Sack On The Smoker

2. Estimate how much thong to use so that the bottom of the smoking skirt will reach the ground with enough extra to pin down. Tie slip knots, so that it they can be easily adjusted.

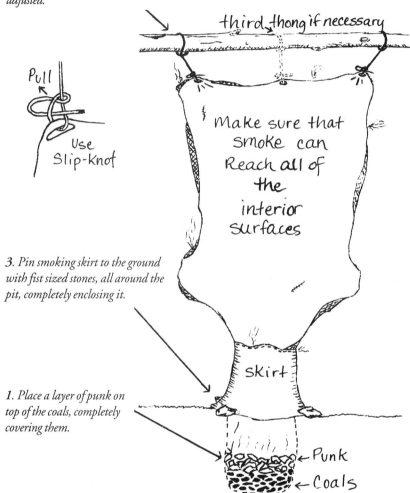

Pull

Use
Slip-Knot

third thong if necessary

make sure that smoke can Reach all of the interior surfaces

3. Pin smoking skirt to the ground with fist sized stones, all around the pit, completely enclosing it.

skirt

1. Place a layer of punk on top of the coals, completely covering them.

←Punk

←Coals

4. Spend some time adjusting and fussing with the hide to make sure that it is lined up straight and the smoke can reach all of the interior surfaces. Smoke should be able to rise in a direct line up through skirt into all areas of the hide sack. There should be no folds, and none of the interior surfaces should be touching one another. Adjust the length and position of the hanging thongs and the way the hide is pinned. Go around the perimeter of the hide making adjustments.

The front cover photo is an example of a hide sack that hangs fairly well. It doesn't have any large ripples or folds, and the top is spread wide. This next shot however is an example of a....

Bad hanging job. *Notice the giant sag and folds in the hide sack. The thongs need to be adjusted so that they pull the upper part of the sack wider. The right thong should also be cinched to raise that side. Hides hung like this will smoke fine functionally, but the color will be extremely uneven.*

Maintaining and Monitoring

From this point on your job is to keep the pit smoking well without it getting too hot. Check the pit every two to four minutes, by

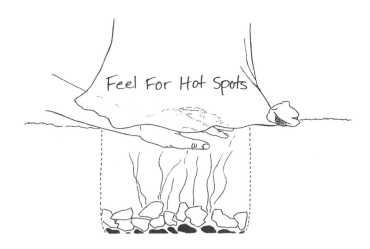

Feel For Hot Spots

lifting the edge of the skirt and putting your hand in to feel for hot spots. Place more punk on any spots that feel particularly hot. The idea is to always have a solid layer of punk over the coals, without adding so much that you smother them. The punk will in turn become coals, and so more punk will need to be added as replacement. Lifting the skirt creates a sudden supply of oxygen and thus a high potential for flare-ups. Don't lift the skirt any higher than necessary and be prepared.

What To Do About Flare-Ups

The main reason you should always be attentive to the smoker is so that you can hear flare-ups. Fire has a distinct roar when it is bursting into being. If you ever hear this roar, grab a handful of punk and put it directly where the flare up is happening. In other words, smother it. Don't panic and don't use water. These flare ups are not very hot...yet. You can easily smother them, with little chance of burning yourself.

READ THIS: If the smoking skirt ever catches fire you have a real problem. Immediately rip the seam that holds the skirt to the hides. Throw the skirt on the ground and put it dead out. It is not worth the risk of burning your hide. (Another option is to tear the hide *and* skirt off of the setup or push the whole setup over. Once the hide and skirt are on the ground then smother or pull the skirt off). Though this happens very rarely you need to be mentally prepared for what to do.

The interior of your hide sack is what is really getting smoked. After ten minutes, you should be able see some color bleeding through the thin spots. At this point, you can start checking the color of the hide to see if it is smoked as dark as you would like it to be. Functionally any color is enough. So from there it is up to you. To check, simply peel open a very short one inch section of your glued seam and look at the interior of the hides. Choose a spot toward the bottom of your sack, as this will be the most lightly colored. The side that you are smoking first is the grain side, and this is generally the side that is worn outward on clothing. Close the hole back up when you are done checking. Smoking this side of the hide typically takes 10 minutes to half an hour, though it can take quite a bit longer if your smoke is weak or the hide is thick. It is generally better to renew the bed of coals than to proceed with wispy smoke. You can also refer to "Factors That Effect Smoking" in the *Tanning Reference* chapter, p. 156.

Smoking The Other Side

When the hide(s) are a color that you want, release the skirt, untie the hanging thongs, and remove your hide sack from the smoking setup. If your hide smoked fairly quickly, place a flat board or piece of metal over the pit to prevent it from flaring up. If it seemed to smoke slowly, allow the pit to remain open so that the coals can heat up and spread.

Turn the entire skirt inside out, first. Then reach up into the sack and grasp the top and pull this out the same way you would a sock. Flipping the skirt first assures that the hide doesn't get stained by contact with the gummy skirt. Be gentle, so that you do not open up the seams. Then rehang the sack and smoke the unsmoked side. Make sure that every section got turned completely inside out, so that it will smoke well. Fuss with the hide(s) to make sure they are lined up well and not touching themselves on the interior. Smoke this side until it is the color you want. This side is typically worn on the inside of clothing.

> DON'T EVER LEAVE YOUR
> SMOKING HIDE UNATTENDED!!!

When Smoking Is Done...

....tear the skirt from the hide(s), pull open the seams and celebrate! Rub your new buckskin all over yourself. Next, rub it all over your friends. Doesn't that feel good?

Billy Metcalf with a stack of finished hides

Variations

There are many other ways to make buckskin. *The Basic Method* is the easiest one that I have ever seen or experienced for most situations. However there are situations in which a different method is more appropriate:

Hides That Have Been Stored Dry a Year or More

Hides that have been cured, intentionally or not, do not need to go through the bucking and rinsing process. By drying out over a long period of time the bound water evaporates, and the mucus breaks down causing the hides to dress and soften easily. The longer the hide is stored the better this works. The grain will also come off easier the longer they are stored. After two or three years the grain comes off as easily as a bucked hide and they soften up great. I don't recommend intentionally pursuing this method as there are too many opportunities for the hide to get ruined by heat, rot, and especially bugs! But if it turns out that Aunt Cecile has three hides stored in the back of the shed from three years ago, this is the way to go. To proceed, soak the hide in plain water for two or three days or until the grain scrapes off easily enough. Omit the rinsing step and the rest is the same.

Changes
+ **Age**
Flesh
~~Buck~~
Grain
~~Rinse~~
Membrane
Brain
Wring
Soften
Smoke

Curing Scraped Rawhide

In this method you omit the bucking and rinsing steps, and dry your hide out after scraping it. This is a more intentional version of the previous variation. The hides tend to cure faster and are not nearly as attractive to bugs. The amount of curing really varies depending on heat and humidity, but is at least several months and usually more like a year plus. You also don't get the advantage of the easy graining that bucking creates. Hides should be soaked in plain water until the grain scrapes off relatively well. This could be one day if the hide was frozen, fresh, or wet-salted. Expect three to ten days for dried hides. This method can be used in combination with the next method, if necessary.

Changes
Flesh
~~Buck~~
Grain
+ Age
~~Rinse~~
Membrane
Brain
Wring
Soften
Smoke

Braining and Rebraining

This method omits the bucking and rinsing and replaces it with doing the wringing and braining steps three or four times. This is the method that I used for years, and was very happy to move on from. However, if for some reason you had no access to wood ashes or lime, or just didn't feel like working with them, it's good to know that this works. The most important skill for this method is to be able to assess when you've wrung and brained the hide enough. This is primarily learned through experience, but you can also use the ripple test as described in the *Dressing* chapter p. 102. Don't bother with this test until you've brained the hide a couple of times or it will fool you.

Changes
Flesh
~~Buck~~
Grain
~~Rinse~~
Membrane
Brain
Wring
+ Brain
+ Wring
+ Brain
+ Wring
Soften
Smoke

For other ideas on this variation see Steven Edholm and Tamara Wilder's *"Buckskin: The Ancient Art of Brain Tanning"*.

Pre-smoking

When you smoke your hide it locks in the softness you've gained and makes it easier to get good brain penetration. Skip the bucking and rinsing. Then after braining, soften the hide, but expect it to stiffen up on you. Once it starts to stiffen up, just let it go stiff. Then smoke it, and just as the hide comes off the smoker and is still damp from the smoke, put it back in the brains. Take it out, work it on the cable, and put it back in the brains. Then wring and soften as usual. The softening will be easier than it would be if you didn't pre-smoke it.

This method has been made popular in recent years by the Dinsmore family of Montana (you can read a more complete description of their method on our website at http://www.braintan.com/articles/presmoke.html).

Changes
Flesh
~~Buck~~
Grain
~~Rinse~~
Membrane
Brain
Wring
+ Soften
+ Smoke
+Brain
+Wring
Soften
~~Smoke~~

Indians in Canada traditionally did this on moose hides. The most common mistake is to smoke it without having brained and softened it once. This results in really tight hides that tear easily. The reason is that smoking creates bridges between the fibers. So if the fibers are physically very close together, then these bridges are really short and they prevent the fibers from being able to separate from one another as much as they should in good buckskin.

I think the best use of this technique is if you follow the basic method (or any other) and the hide comes out stiff. Smoking the hide before rebraining and resoftening will make it more likely that the hide comes out just right the second time, and will make the second round of softening easier. This is especially valuable with big thick hides like elk, moose and buffalo which are harder to get good brain penetration with, and are a lot of work to soften.

Infinite combinations of these methods can and are used by various tanners to create buckskin. What is important to understand is how to get the grain loose enough to remove without undue pain, and how to get the brains to penetrate. Remember that brains can not magically penetrate through the hide and its protective mucus on their own.

Other Techniques.

Other techniques that can help brain penetration include:

Freezing the brained hide. Multiple freezing and thawing of brained hides seems to improve brain penetration.

Dry scraping. Many folks dry their fleshed hides on a rack and then shear off the grain and upper part of the fiber network to below the hair roots. This gets down to where the fibers are larger and there is very little mucus, allowing relatively easy brain penetration. This is the way the Plains Indians tanned their buffalo hides (though they typically soaked them in a wood ash solution first). For a complete guide see Jim Riggs' *"Blue Mountain Buckskin...A working manual to dry-scrape brain tan"*.

I've heard of people who put their dressed hides in washing machines to improve penetration. Somehow all of the agitation and centrifugal force accomplishes much of the same job as wringing and dressing a whole bunch of times. This is basically how modern oil tans are done (though in combination with liming, rinsing and an open air heating step).

Infinite combinations of these methods can and are used by various tanners to create buckskin. What is important to understand is how to get the grain loose enough to remove without undue pain, and how to get the brains to penetrate. Remember that brains can not magically penetrate through the mucus on their own.

Going Further

Tanning Reference

Here are more details about each of the different steps in the process to help you better understand the mechanics of tanning. This information is unnecessary for tanning your first hide, but can be very useful in the long run. It will help you to trouble shoot, tan hides in batches, and bring out certain qualities in the buckskin (even smoke, knappier surface, less knappy surface, etc.). It also tells you how to vary the basic method to suit different climates, seasons and situations.

Fleshing

It is easier to *deeply* flesh once the hair and grain cushion is removed from the other side. However, in order to remove the hair and grain, we need to remove the strips and lumps of meat and fat from the flesh side. We'll come back for the membrane later, when we can get it *all* easily. Most people waste time over-fleshing at this juncture. Since you *have* to come back for the deeper layers of membrane you should leave all you can for then. It is so much easier to get once the hair is gone!

Bucking

The Factors That Affect Soaking Time

Strength. The alkali in wood ashes are small enough that they can become concentrated in the water beyond the appropriate strength. If *really* strong they start attacking the fibers and eventually dissolve them. Weaker solutions don't work very well, even if you soak the hide for a really long time, even if the hair is totally falling out. The hides swell and scrape easily, but the mucus isn't loosened sufficiently, and will still inhibit penetration by the dressing. I think of it as a kind of gang up affect. If there are enough alkali (OH- ions), their combined pull on the hydrogen bonds is strong enough to dislodge them, but if there are not enough around the bonds will stay intact and the mucus will continue its filtration job, resulting in poor brain penetration. I've experimented with this considerably and found the old pioneer recipe (floating an egg in the ash lye) to be perfect! This allows a boundary of safety that does not harm the fibers but thoroughly cleans out the mucus.

This line of safety is similar to that of using different temperatures of water to soak hides. At temperatures up to 110 degrees it is totally safe and speeds absorption. At 150 degrees the skin gets cooked and falls apart. One is *totally* safe, but above a certain point it is *totally* unsafe.

There is a small window of opportunity in which one can get the mucus removal benefits of bucking without having to rinse or neutralize the hide. This occurs when the solution is on the weak side, in the low 12's on pH paper. An egg will typically sink slowly or hover just below the surface of the solution. I chased this window for quite a while, because it meant one less step to do. But after doing a lot of hides I decided that this window is too small to find consistently. Too many hides needed to be rebrained or just barely came out soft enough. The stronger solutions are much easier to get right, make the scraping substantially easier, and the hides consistently come out great. I don't recommend trying work within this window, and just look at it as backup when you accidentally make the solution a bit too weak.

PH paper or egg floating...which is more scientific? Alkalinity is measured on a pH scale of 1 to 14, 7 being neutral, 1 very acidic and 14 way alkaline. This scale is 'exponential', meaning that 9 is ten times as alkaline as 8, and so on. The pH that an egg floats at is approximately 12.9-13.0. This may sound really strong, but it is only because the scale is exponential. If the scale were 1 to 10, zero being neutral, then a pH of 13.0 would be equal to 1. I think because most substances fall within this lower range of pH that they made the scale exponential to be able to measure these more accurately. The pH that we use (13.0) is as alkaline as lemon juice is acidic. There are high-tech tools that will measure this accurately. Regular pH paper does not. It will only tell you that the pH is 12 rather than 11. 12.9 is nine *times* as potent as 12.1. This is a huge difference, the difference between ineffective and very effective. An egg is much more accurate. Probably the most extreme variation you could find in egg density is two to one. This is a much smaller margin of error than the nine to one of pH paper. White hormone pumped eggs are much less dense and float easily. The old recipe is based on using hearty homegrown eggs, so use the most natural ones you can find. Egg sized potatoes are also reputed to work but I have little experience with them.

Temperature. Activity slows down the colder it is. In very cold weather allow one extra day of soaking. Don't count any time that the hide spends frozen.

Time. It takes time for the alkalinity to penetrate and make the mucus water soluble. Skin is a tightly woven structure and the alkali must deconstruct the mucus as it goes, in order to penetrate farther.

Thickness. The thicker the skin, the longer it takes for the alkali to penetrate fully. Really thick hides should be soaked an extra day.

Stirring. The more often the hide is stirred around in the solution, the faster the alkali penetrate. The recipe given in *The Basic Method* section assumes no stirring. If you stir, it will take less time. This is because the hide is absorbing the alkali that are right on the surface of the hide. As these alkali are absorbed, the quantity of alkali that are available decrease. More alkali will move over toward the depleted areas next to the hide. This is how alkali behave in a solution. This movement can be greatly speeded up by stirring the hide and the solution. If you are in a hurry to scrape your hide, put it in a warm place, and stir frequently. Commercial tanneries use vats with paddle wheels, and 70 degree temp., to get their lime solutions to fully penetrate in 24 hours.

Learning to Be Efficient

Each type of wood will consistently yield the same strength ash. Get to know the approximate ratio of ash to water that is right for the type of wood you burn. That way you won't need to readjust the solution.

Your ash water is an important resource. Reuse any extra solution, and hand wring excess from the hide back into solution, when you remove the hide. *This cuts way down on ash consumption.* I would estimate that each hide consumes one gallon or less of wood-ash. We use a large wooden barrel or plastic trash can, make a big solution, get it right and put four to six hides in at once, and then reuse it many times. This is definitely more efficient than making new solutions every time you tan a hide.

Graining

The Guide To Easier Scraping

These are some of the variables that effect how hard it is to remove the grain from a skin.

Hide Storage. It is easiest to degrain fresh, wet-salted or frozen hides. If dried for storage, and reconstituted to scrape, the grain will be harder to remove, getting easier the longer it is soaked. See *Storing Hides*, p. 50.

Area of contact between beam and scraping tool. The less area of contact between your beam and scraping tool, the more your force is concentrated and the easier the grain is removed. The narrower and more steeply rounded your beam is the easier the grain will come off, but the more often you will need to readjust the hide, on the small working surface. If your tool is rounded (like an ulna-radius) you need an even steeper arc on your beam. See beams p. 60.

Age and sex of skin. A younger deer's grain is generally easier to remove than an older deer's. Does are generally easier to degrain than bucks, especially their necks. Sometimes the lowest levels of grain are harder to fully remove from younger skins. This may be because that layer is less developed and hasn't separated as distinctly from the fiber core. This layer will not inhibit brain penetration but will inhibit smoke, leaving a whiter surface wherever it was left, creating a hazy or streaky appearance.

Sharpness of tool. Distinct edges grip better and remove grain more easily. You want a distinct edge, but a dull one. Too sharp and you can easily cut the hide and leave a gouged or scratched up surface. Using a "sharper" edge to ease scraping is not worth the trade-offs in gouges and scrape marks. There are better routes to easier scraping. The ideal is to get your edge sharp, in our classic understanding of the term, and then dull it a good bit from there. I've never experienced bone tools being too sharp. See the scraper's edge p. 56.

Firmness of beam. Any give, or bounce in your beam, will absorb your energy, detouring it from your scraping. See beams p. 59.

Acidifying

I wouldn't pretend that I know exactly why acidifying your hide works, but it probably has something to do with de-naturing the mucus some more, or changes it causes to the collagen fibers themselves. Most leather tanning methods include some version of this, though it is frequently called 'deliming'. 'Pickling' is another common tanning technique involving acids, but it uses much stronger acids, and is really more of an acidic version of bucking (it cleans out the mucus), that is used on hair-on hides and furs.

Parameters. If you drop the ph too low it will start to swell on the acid side and become 'pickled'. This is harmless, but it will get in the way of brain penetration, so you'll need to bring the hide back toward neutral. You know you've gone too far when the hide becomes swollen and rubbery just like it did when bucking. It is okay if it becomes a little swollen here and there as long as it doesn't get rubbery. If you make the hide a bit too acid (but not pickled), the hide will come out nice and soft but the fibers will have a slightly harsh feel to them. None of this will normally happen to you. I just wanted to relay the results of my experiments to answer the question "if a little acid is good, is more better?".

Membraning

Exactly how much membrane do you need to remove? In the softening stage, sheets of membrane will dry before the underlying layers of hide. The sheets will then contract and prevent these layers from stretching fully. The underlying skin will soften just fine though, and you could just break up the sheets of membrane during the softening stage. This is fairly straight forward to do if you are frame-softening, just scrape it off with an edged tool. My friends at River Spirit do this and it works just fine. The surface becomes covered with soft, fluffy stuff. When hand softening, membrane removal is more of a pain in the butt, unless you have pumice.

The other reason to remove membrane is that these "sheets" will inhibit smoke penetration, creating "blotchy" coloring. I like blotchy coloring, but if it's important to you to have it look even, be sure to remove most of the membrane.

Some folks believe that membrane will inhibit brain penetration. I believe this to be true only to the degree that it tends to keep the hide wetter underneath. Membrane on its own does not inhibit brain penetration. Many hundreds of beautiful hides have been tanned without removing one blot of membrane prior to braining. So the membrane needs to be removed, but you could do it now or later. I find it is easier to remove wet on the beam.

Summary of choices. You can membrane extremely thoroughly and it will reduce the amount of fuzz on the back of your hides, and push more moisture out. You also have a chance to remove more of this membrane and fuzz during the softening process. Some folks love the fuzz, and some don't—your choice. It is soft and fluffy, but tends to dry with hard tips after wetting. These tips can be scratchy unless you abrade them off.

Dressing

Some folks put completely dry hides into the brains. Not only does this take longer for the hide to soak up the solution, but it doesn't brain very well because the oils can't penetrate through the fiber glues (which is what makes hides dry hard and stiff and the dressing is supposed to inhibit, by the opposite action: glues have a hard time setting up through a coat of oil). I did this for some time, thinking that all the moisture in the hide would be brain juice and thus more effective. It just isn't. It leads to rebraining, or half-tanned hides. I finally figured this out. Most people realize the folly of this method fairly quickly. It is a seemingly logical route to take, but don't bother. Putting your hide into the brains dry, and then wringing it out and rebraining is a fine and effective braining method, though not necessarily any better than simply wringing and braining. I don't think its worth the effort of trying to cram a dry hide down into a bucket.

Wringing

Wringing has an inherent drawback. No matter what method you use to wring, your hide will be wrung unevenly. Most of your hide will be perfectly wrung out, but some spots will almost always be wetter than ideal. These spots are the thicker areas and the areas that are on the edges of the hide, especially the neck, butt cheeks and edges that stick out from the main body (flaps). Because these areas (with the exception of the butt cheeks) are on the edges, they can slip and adjust rather than be torqued by the process of wringing.

The way to remedy this is to wring the hide out thoroughly and then go to the beam and use your scraper to push the excess water out of the spots that did not get wrung well. In this way the wringing takes care of the bulk of the hide and squeegeeing does the detail work.

Damping Back (instead of wringing)

If you dried your hide out after braining, damping back can be a simple way to get the hide moist enough for softening, without having to wring. It is particularly effective with hides that had to be rebrained, and now need to be softened again. These rebrained hides readily absorb moisture and can easily be stretched open when only a little damp.

Basic Damping Back

Place the hide in a body of water that is big enough that you do not need to fold your hide in any way to get it in. A creek, river, pond, puddle, lake, or large tub will work fine for this. If the body of water you are using is moving, place a rock or two on your hide so it doesn't go down stream (whoops!). If its not moving it will sink to the bottom and stay there. Leave hide in water for half an hour to two hours, depending on thickness. The neck will be the slowest place to soak up, once it is pliable, the rest of your hide will be plenty soaked up. A good test is to take a spot on the neck and give it a little stretch, if it will stretch at all, then it is ready. Do this test only on the neck, because anywhere you stretch and re-soak will become sopping wet. For your first time, err on the wetter side. Also, in hotter weather, it is good to have a little more moisture.

Take your hide out of the water and lay or hang it in a shady place if its a hot day, or in the sun on a cool day. You want to allow all of the surface moisture to evaporate. Any surface water that doesn't evaporate will soak into your hide when you stretch it open, making it unnecessarily wet. This should take two to ten minutes. Keep an eye on it.

Next, stretch your hide open, in all directions. Ideally, it should be white and stretchy everywhere. If the neck and butt cheeks are hard to hand stretch open, you need to break them open over an edge. The staking tool is designed especially for this. If you don't have a staking tool setup, use any edge that will work: the corner of a chair, your porch, car door, a stump, whatever!

Once your hide is white and stretchy everywhere, sew any holes and continue on into the stretching routine...

Alternatives for Rainy, Foggy and Dewy Conditions

These weather conditions can provide the perfect dampness to get your hide ready for softening, with no extra moisture. This can be very efficient because the moisture level is so low and even, that you are immediately at the softening stage that matters, throughout the hide. You can focus your energy on stretching and buffing for a shorter time, and be done. They are also excellent for cooler times of the year, when it takes longer to soften. There is a fine line between enough moisture and not enough, so try this only when you have the experience to know what a softening hide should feel like. You will be amazed just how little moisture it takes.

These methods will not work if your hide is not brained well. Try them only after you have convinced yourself that you have the braining thing down. If you do have a rebrained hide, these methods work even better, as the hides are easier to work soft, due to their previous softening experience.

Preparation. After braining, dry the brains into the hide.

Absorbing moisture. Next, your hides need to absorb enough moisture to be able to work them from damp to dry.

Rainy season. When dry, hang it out in the woodshed, as close to the edge as possible without it getting rained on at all. If it is windy this method won't work, but if there is a steady rain, by morning your hide will be damp, just slightly. Pull on a thin spot. If it will stretch open, soft and white, it is probably ready. The harder it is raining the moister your hide will be. Be very careful not to allow any rain to get on the hide.

Dewing it. Hang your dried hide out where it will soak in a lot of dew. This method will work only in areas that have a lot of dew. Dew is heavier in cold sinks, where cold air settles on clear nights. These same areas are frost pockets in really cold weather. Also, look for places that are protected from breezes but otherwise very exposed and open to the night sky. The hide collects more dew if it is horizontal rather than vertical, but do not lay it directly on the ground or grass or it will get too wet in spots. Work the hide open first thing in the morning, before the sun hits, or it will get too dry.

You need to have a predictably heavy dew to even bother with this one. I used to live in a river canyon that got heavy dew for half of the year, almost every night. This made this method very effective, and a lot of fun. Where I live now doesn't seem to get hard enough dew to make it worth it.

Fog. I've never actually used fog to damp back a hide, but I have no doubt that it would work. If you get a heavy fog, try this one out. I think it could be the best situation of the bunch.

Stretching the hide open. Work in an unheated space. You don't want the hide to start drying until you have it fully opened, stretchy, and any holes sewed. You need to have a ground stake to do this (see p. 178). Stretch the hide open over the stake, section by section. This can be tedious, depending on the moisture content. When every spot is worked open, soft, and white go to the cable. Cable the membrane side by dividing the hide into thirds and working it methodically in all directions. Flip over and cable the hair side the same way. Cable until it all feels good.

Once the hide is fully opened, sew any holes and then bring the hide into the sun or a heated space and work the hide as usual until it is dry and rebounding. If most of the hide feels good, but some spots are hopelessly stiff, then it means it wasn't brained well. If brained well, these spots will always stretch open. Stick it back in some brains, while there is still moisture in the hide.

Discussion. Once the holes are sewed, the drying and working in a heated space is not very labor intensive, nor does it take long. You can work two hides at once by doing all of the previous steps in the moist outdoor air, and then bring them both into the sun or heated space when they are ready. They will not start drying until you do.

If you ever feel like you can't keep up with the rate of drying, and it is raining, you can simply put the hide(s) back out in the shed, and they will stop drying, and begin to reabsorb moisture. You can also bag them in a plastic bag.

Basically, if you can create the perfect humidity for your hide to damp back in, you can get it uniformly to the necessary moisture content for softening, and no more, every time. This would be the ideal way to prepare hides for softening. This ideal *is* available from the skies above, but at their discretion.

Sewing Holes

The easiest time to sew holes is when the hide has reached the white and stretchy stage of softening but is still damp. Don't try this out until you've become proficient at softening though. It's a bit trickier making sure the hide doesn't dry out too much.

Factors That Affect The Ease Of Sewing:

Wetness of hide. The dryer your hide is when you sew, the easier it is to push the needle through, but the more liable the hide is to dry too much in the course of sewing. For your first hides, sew holes right after wringing. If a hole is sopping wet, then squeegee moisture out of that area, on the beam. When you become more proficient, you can sew your holes when the hide is drier. The lack of moisture and separateness of the fibers allows the needle to slip through more easily. By this time in the softening process, the edges around the hole will have stiffened up some. Work them really good, and then clip off anything that won't loosen up. I don't recommend this timing for beginners because typically they need to spend more time sewing and their hides dry out too much. If you wait too long the fibers will not realign and flatten the hole. Anytime before the area surrounding the hole shows signs of "rebounding" is fine. I like to sew holes when the hide is in the white and stretchy stage.

How well the edge of the hole is dressed. If the edge of your hole is well-dressed, the needle can easily slide through the fibers. If it is not well dressed, the inner structure will be tight, making it harder to push the needle through. Dressings provide an oily film that helps separate the fibers. The edge of holes, like the edge of the hide, is frequently poorly brained. I'm not sure why this is. Perhaps moisture gets stuck there in the dressing preparation step, or we forget to pull the edges when dressing. Trim any stiff edges before sewing.

Softening

Other Basic Softening Tools

Staking posts are excellent stretching tools and can have metal implanted in their tips to make them better abraders. They are great for helping put your weight into the stretching. These tools are also the best for opening up damped back hides (see damping back p. 149). Makeshift staking posts include the corners on chairs, fence posts, etc.

Hafted stone or metal. These tools are similar to the beveled tools except a piece of stone or metal has been inserted in the tip. Stone and metal hold an edge better than antler, bone or wood, and so make a better abrading tool with less maintenance. Do not use an edge sharp enough to cut. Some stones to try out are those in the flint family and slate.

Learning to Be Efficient

As you gain experience, you come to understand when and where a hide needs to be worked. It doesn't need to be worked constantly. It does need to be worked *thoroughly* periodically. How periodically depends on how fast it is drying. If it's 100 degrees and you're in full sun, it is best to work constantly and your hide will be done quickly. In 50 degrees and overcast, periodically means working your hide for five to ten minutes every twenty to thirty minutes and it'll be four to five hours until your hide is done. Have other projects to do or soften three hides at once. When you get really proficient you can soften two hides at once, in full sun, and take some breaks. I almost always soften two hides at once. The key is to be methodical. Work all sections of the hide once. Then do the same to the other hide. The first one will dry just enough to be ready for another round of stretching.

Whatever shape your hide is in as it dries will influence its final shape. If your hide is constantly scrunched up on the cable, it will dry smaller, thicker and with a slightly scrunched appearance (elephant grain). If it spends a lot of time stretched out wide—it will dry wider; stretched out long—it will dry longer. If it is stretched on a frame it can be stretched bigger, flat and thinner. The hide will readjust *toward* its original shape, when it gets wet for the first time after smoking. However, it will permanently retain some of the size and shape you softened and smoked it in.

Learning From Stiff Spots

Was stiffness the result of incomplete bucking, poor brain penetration or not working the hide enough during softening?

Stiffness caused by incomplete mucus removal follows a very definite pattern. If your hide is stiff in these areas and soft everywhere else, then it is almost definite that the bucking was incomplete. If these areas are soft, but other places are stiff, then it is surely not the bucking, but either imperfect moisture content at the moment of immersion into the dressing, or not working those areas appropriately.

You can also learn about the source of your stiffness by cutting a section of stiff hide. Usually the most convenient place to cut is up at the top of the neck. You need only take a snip. Then look at the interior of the skin. Typically the outer layers will appear fibery and well fluffed. If the interior is a hard yellow line, with no fibrousness to it, it means that the alkali did not fully remove the mucus. If the center is white and a bit fibrous, but highly compacted, then brains never reached that area (usually it was too wet or dry when put in brains) or you stopped working it before it was really dry.

Think back...was this area wetter than ideal when it was stuck in the brains? Or do you remember quitting the softening process a little earlier than was ideal, or somehow let that spot dry before it was really worked?

Frame Softening vs. Hand Softening

Deer hides, especially large ones were softened on a frame by a large portion of Native American tribes. Many other peoples softened their hides by hand. Some did both. Here are the pros and cons.

Advantages Of Frame Softening

* You see all sections of the hide at once.

* You can stretch the hide larger and thinner, though you lose stretchiness in the finished product. It is also more likely to shrink when washed, so wash before making clothing. However, a large portion of the size gained, and the thinning, are permanent.

* The hide is held in place so you just have to think about working it with the staker tool, rather than supporting its weight or needing to hold it to provide resistance to the hand tool work.

* It is a very comfortable way to work heavy hides.

* The finished hide lies flat, making pattern cutting extra easy.

* Hide is fully exposed to all drying elements, at all times, drying faster.

* It is a little less demanding on your hands and wrists, which is important if you are at risk to get carpel tunnel syndrome.

Disadvantages Of Frame Softening

* Have to build frame and have lots of cordage.

* Its easy and almost inevitable to stretch hides into an unnatural shape, which invites shrinkage and shape changing problems, later. However, most if not all of these problems *can* be prevented by wetting and drying your hides after smoking, before cutting into them.

* Hide dries while lacing on frame, so unless hide is a bit moister, or you take care to do it quickly in a cool place, it can get too dry.

* You are much more likely to break through and create holes. This

will happen only in already weak spots, but your tool will make the hole as big as itself, as it slides through.

* A frame is not nearly as portable to beautiful places, in and out of sun and shade, wind and rain.

* If your hide is not brained well and starts stiffening, it takes five minutes to take it down after you notice, causing your hide to dry more and not rebrain as well.

* Once started you are committed until its done. Most plastic bags will not fit over a frame.

Smoking

Color Control?

While certain types of punk tend to give certain colors, you can never have absolute control over the color that you are going to get. Using just Douglas fir punk I have gotten golden, bronze, lemon yellow, burnt orange, rich brown, and pukey green. Sometimes I have wildly different colors, using the exact same punk stash on the same day. The color seems to depend on the moisture content of the punk, how hot the smoke is, how decayed the tree is, the phase of the moon, and what type of decay (dry rot, wet rot, cold rot, blue rot, hot rot, shoe rot...where is Dr. Seuss when you need him?). *My* strategy and I think it's a good one, is to smoke the hide and enjoy whatever color it gives me!

Factors That Effect Smoking

(A) The more the smoke goes directly into the hide sack and is *trapped* there, the faster the hide smokes:

Air tight stoves, cans and pits are more efficient than drafty stoves that lose smoke through the seams.

The less porous the skirt material, the less smoke you lose through it. Using no skirt at all is possible with the pit. This is the most efficient, because you are only smoking the hide, not the skirt material too. Though you are more likely to get the hide dirty.

The **tightness of your sack seams**. The tighter your sack seams the more smoke is trapped in the sack. Rather than leaving through the seams, pressure builds up and smoke enters the hide faster. Ideally the pressure in the sack will cause it to "balloon".

(B) The more smoke created, the faster the hide smokes. These factors increase the quantity of smoke:

The quality of the coal bed. Coals should be strong at the start and uniformly covering the base of your pit or stove. The damper your punk, the more important this is.

The quantity of punk. Always have enough punk in the pit to completely cover the coals, and then some. Put on a little extra punk, if the punk is damp, so it can be drying out. Too much punk can smother.

The quality of the punk and its application. Chunky punk creates more air spaces allowing the coals to be hot and make the punk smoke. Fine punk, flour to oats consistency, smothers. It is useful to have on hand if the smudge is generally too hot and you need to cool it off. Otherwise it slows the smoking down.

The volume of the pit or stove. The bigger it is the more volume of coals and punk it can handle, and thus the more smoke it can produce. However, the more fuel there is the hotter any flare ups can get.

Moose, Elk, Caribou, Antelope & Goat

Moose, elk, caribou, antelope and goat can be tanned by similar means as deer, with the following differences:

Antelope

Pronghorn antelope are generally much thinner than deer. Use less pressure scraping the grain and membrane off, and don't wring them as hard or else you might tear holes. They also have a pair of glands on either side of the backbone, near the tail, that inevitably will result in extremely thin spots or holes. There is nothing you can do about this except be aware of them so that you don't tear these areas into larger holes than need be.

Pronghorn hides are surprisingly strong despite their thinness. This combination results in finished hides that are highly valued for lightweight yet tough clothing. They are great for cruising the woods in warm weather, or for elegant ladies' dresses. Pronghorn also have a noticeably 'tighter' fiber texture than do deer. They don't get as stretchy soft.

Elk

Elk are generally much thicker than deer, but have a weaker fiber structure. Much to most people's surprise, a pair of deer skin moccasins will usually outlast a pair made of elk. You'll see this in the course of tanning—the fibers are bigger, coarser, and have more of a tendency to pull apart. Still, for most uses, elk will last a lifetime, provides a huge expanse of material and is worth your time tanning.

   You should have a couple of deer under your belt before you attempt tanning an elk. Every part of the elk tanning process takes longer. They need to soak in the buck longer for the alkali to penetrate all the way to the center. They also need to rinse longer, in order to get all of the alkali back out. The thickness of elk hide makes it dry slower, so softening takes longer. Here are some specific recommendations:

Bucking

Soak elk hides until they have become fully swollen and tawny, and then leave them two more days, just to make sure the alkali penetrate all the way to the center.

Rinsing

Rinse the alkali out of elk hides until they have lost all signs of being swollen, and then rinse for 24 hrs. longer, just to make sure it all rinses out.

Wringing

It is hard to get elk hides to wring out well, because they are so thick. It helps to use a much longer wringing stick, for added leverage. Still, you will probably have areas that don't wring out very well.

Acidifying

Do it. The real benefit here is that it will allow you to brain the hide while totally dry, giving you complete brain penetration in one fell swoop. I'm not saying that every elk hide will come out soft in one braining, but if everything is done correctly and completely, that does indeed happen. And because thick hides take so long to soften, and are otherwise considerably more difficult to get good brain penetration with, I can comfortably state that acidifying will cut your overall tanning time in half. Acidify your elk hides for twice as long as you would deer.

Dressing

Use twice as much dressing as you would for deer. Wring and dress the hide at least twice before attempting to soften it.

Eric Susee & Hec Morton with their first Elk

Softening

A lot of tanners prefer to frame soften elk, because they are so heavy. They also tend to dry a lot faster on the frame. If you hand soften, set up your cable so that most of the weight of the hide is resting on something (like the ground, or a tarp on the ground).

It is even more important with thick hides to work in a well-heated space. If it's warm enough, your elk will dry in 6-8 hrs., if it's not, it can take days.

The thicker areas, such as the neck and rumps, may feel dry on the exterior, but still be wet on the interior. Don't be fooled into thinking the hide is done, only to have those areas stiffen as they dry. Work the hide until you are absolutely sure those areas are dry, and then come check in on them every hour or two to make sure they aren't stiffening.

If your hide doesn't come soft the first time (which is likely), make it into a simple smoking sack by folding it lengthwise along the spine and threading string through the holes used on the frame. Hang it over your smoker like you would a deer and smoke it until it gets some color. Have your dressing warm and ready and put the hide in *immediately* when it comes off the smoker. You want the hide to be a bit damp from the smoke as it helps the hide better absorb the solution. Then wring and dress it again before attempting your next softening. This 'pre-smoking' will lock in the softness you have already achieved and make it dry faster and easier the next time around.

Moose

Moose are usually very thick too, but they are much stronger fibered than elk. Historically, wherever moose hides were available for moccasins, they were used. Moose should be tanned the same way as elk. The only real difference is the moose's hump. This area is harder to scrape because it won't lay flat, and it is very hard to get soft. I've encountered humps that I just chose to give up on, even though the rest of the hide was buttery soft.

Moose hide makes the most durable moccasins.

Goat

Goats are very similar to pronghorn antelope (they're related). They have the same tight fiber structure, tend to be thin and are relatively strong. They are a good substitute for deer when none are available.

Caribou

I've never done a caribou myself, but they are known to be thin, strong, and relatively easy to tan. Summer hides typically have little holes all over them from warbles. On winter hides, these holes have healed up and become little areas of circular white tissue.

Nature's Tools

There is something deeply satisfying about tanning a hide with tools that you have produced from forest and field. To create your own clothes from just what nature has to offer you, to be comfortable with the tools and materials that she provides, is inspiring, liberating, and downright fun! It may also surprise you to learn that it is barely any harder to do. In fact one can tan a hide just as quickly with primitive tools as with modern ones. The efficiency of one's tanning method is more important than the materials from which the tools are made.

The main challenge is in taking the time to learn how to work with unfamiliar materials. Once the tools are made, the difference is that the scrapers and some softening tools will dull faster and therefore require more maintenance. Most of the time this is just a minute or two here and there. However, with hard to scrape hides the additional pressure that is required can dull primitive scrapers quickly causing a constant need to rework the edge. This can be a real pain. It should however be a rare problem if hides are properly stored and soaked. Storing and bucking the hide correctly are really key. Primitive tools will also wear out and new ones need to be produced. This is where metal has its big advantage.

There are many different ways one can approach tanning with natural tools. There is the survivalist/adventurer who wants to know how to do it in the wilderness after just killing a deer. There are those who just like the feel of doing things with no modern or industrial implements, or even want to live that way. Some folks want to recreate an authentic Native American tanning experience in order to learn more about their life ways and material culture. Hopefully this chapter can provide enough information for you to successfully adapt to any of these scenarios. Use the same Basic Method described previously.

Most of the following information comes from studying accounts of Native American tanning, personal experience and experiments, as well as teaching and learning from students and friends. It is an area of tanning that I am particularly fascinated with. If you come up with any interesting tools, innovations or ideas I would love to hear from you.

Storing Brains

Brains have this nasty habit of rotting. If you've never squished green, rotting brains between your fingers, then you've got to try it. Fortunately I've already had this important life experience and am ready to move on. The solution for many Native American tribes was to mix the extra brains with various fibrous materials, and then dry them. Brains do not dry very well on their own. They tend to get an outer skin, which seals in moisture and causes them to rot. Fibrous materials absorb the brains and break up their mass into little bits that dry easily. I've read about people using moss, sagebrush bark, yucca fibers, and fine grasses. Anything fibrous and a bit absorbent should work. I use the green moss that grows thick on tree trunks and rocks. You can add sprigs of plants that have a pleasant smell. The hide will pick up the scent and release it as it is softened. Try sage, cedar, pine, mints, rose, ... whatever your nose enjoys.

Making Brain Patties

Start with a fiber wad that is about four times as big as the brains that you plan to dry. More is better and it does take more than you'd think. Massage the brains into some of the moss. Keep adding moss until all of the brains are soaked up and you don't see any more clumps. At this point the moss will feel oily. Press the moss into as thin of a patty as you can, while keeping it in one piece. One inch thick works well. Dry in the sun, over a fire or in the oven. It is no problem if the patty cooks.

It takes a certain leap of faith to trust that these funny dried things will work, but they do! The longest that I've stored them so far was six months and they worked just fine. They probably can be stored much longer. The other great advantage is that there is no risk of rotting, in storage or transit. If you have moss or similar fibrous material, this is an extremely simple and effective way to store and re-soak your brains.

Michelle holds moss and brains. Massage the two together, shape, then dry. Five finished patties hang from above. The uninitiated may mistake them for cow chips so keep an eye on your stash.

To use, place the patty in a container (this container is a hide laid in a depression) with the appropriate amount of hot water. Massage brains out of moss as much as possible. The soup should become milky. Remove moss, wringing excess moisture back into the soup. You can reuse the moss or discard it wantonly.

Bucking

Bucking can be done in any type of wooden container. Log troughs were very commonly used by Native American tribes. You could also try large pottery containers or pits in the ground that have been baked hard — like a smoking pit in clay soil. To measure the strength of hardwood ash solutions there may be some natural starchy bulbed plant in your area that has the right specific gravity. Experiment with yucca, soaproot, camas or any other large lilies. The best technique in a 'survival' situation would be to already have a good feel for the proper thickness of hard wood ash solutions or to use soft wood ashes and make it thick.

Bucking can also be done by spreading the hide out on the ground and smearing ashes and water onto both surfaces. Then roll the hide up and bury it in the ground to keep it moist. Try to do it in a way that keeps the solution in contact with the hide. I wouldn't worry about making the solution too strong in this case, as you will inevitably lose some. (I've only done this twice. One worked great, one didn't. The difference seems to have been whether or not the juice drained off of the hide or not). Several hides could be done in this way by laying them out one on top of another.

As always, it is extremely important to do this step well, as it sets up the ease of scraping and brain penetration that make all the difference in tanning. Make sure the solution is the right strength, that the hide gets thoroughly coated and that it soaks long enough.

Scraping

Beams

Beams can be made from downed trees, branches and driftwood. You can burn off the jagged ends. Although it is slower, hides can be scraped on a very narrow two to three inch wide beam when necessary. The working surface can be smoothed by scraping with broken rocks or grinding with sandstone.

Using Primitive Scrapers

The ideal scraper should have:

A straight working edge. Curved edges at first look advantageous because they conform to the shape of the beam. However for this very reason, they disperse your force over a wider surface, making it harder to get a good grip on the flesh, grain, or membrane. If you do use a curved edge, like on an ulna radius, use it with a narrower, sharply rounded beam, to compensate.

The ability to hold a distinct edge. You do not want a sharp edge, but a distinct one. One that can grip and be pushed between the layers of skin. A sharp one will cut too deep. An overly dull scraper will require more force from you to effectively remove the grain. Bone is an excellent material for scrapers. It holds its edge reasonably well, is easy to sharpen, and will never get too sharp. Hard woods can also work well, though they tend to dull faster. Stone can be used but you must be careful to avoid sharp or jagged edges.

Big cushy comfortable handles. While this may seem like a luxury, it is really very functional. Comfortable handles allow you to exert maximum force. If your hands are sore there is an inevitable tendency to hold back on pressure, causing you to miss grain, take more strokes (which are increasingly painful) and scrape less efficiently.

This primitive scraper is made from a buffalo hump vertebra. Notice the cushy moss handles. Wads of moss have been lashed around the bone with a buckskin thong. The texture of the moss helps prevent it from slipping around. Adding these soft handles to my bone scraper made a big difference.

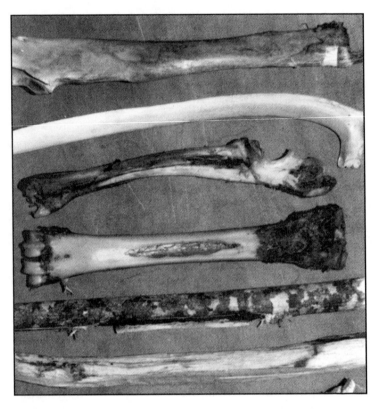

A Sampling of Scrapers—used for fleshing and graining. Top to bottom:

__Thoraxic vertebrae, buffalo__. This is one of the vertebrae that form the buffalo's hump. Very flat, stout tool, with natural edge.

__Rib, buffalo__. Pretty good tool. Steaming and straightening makes it more comfortable to use.

__Ulna-radius, deer__. Natural edge. Don't over clean, as sinewy membranes hold it together. Use narrower beam.

__Cannon bone beamer, elk__. Two edges created by hollowing out center.

__Wood and bone scraper__. Bone shard implanted in wood with pitch binder.

__Split stick, oak__. Various hardwoods.

Materials:

Bone. Bone was the most common scraping tool of the Native Americans. It is easy to sharpen and impossible to get too sharp. Its lone drawback is that it dulls faster than steel. Eventually they will wear out completely, needing to be replaced. Luckily, every deer comes with more than you need.

Wood. Wooden scrapers were used by some Native Americans. Woods that I have tried do not hold an edge well enough to scrape a hide. However, I think that very hard woods would. A buddy of mine named John Mein has successfully scraped a number of hides using a piece of black locust. Also if you use a narrower beam, the distinctness of your edge becomes correspondingly less crucial. So, in a pinch you should be able to use any moderately hard wood on a narrow (three inch or less) round beam.

Stone. Stone was rarely used for traditional wet scraping tools, but certain ones may work fine. The first stone I would bother trying is slate. It is hard and can be ground to a clean edge. Flake-able stones such as flint, chert, basalt etc., should work, especially if you simply snap a pancake shaped one in half, rather than flaking it. Obsidian may be too brittle and prone to jagged edges. Once the blank is made, be sure to grind those edges smooth and a bit dull. Then haft to a comfortable wooden drawknife. Stone scrapers are more laborious to make, but should hold their edge better than bone or wood. I don't have much experience with this.

HOW TO SHARPEN BONE HIDE SCRAPERS

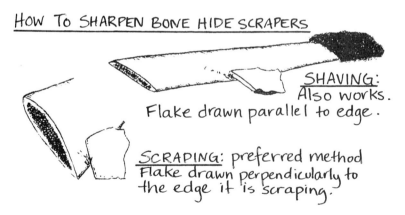

SHAVING: Also works.
Flake drawn parallel to edge.

SCRAPING: preferred method
Flake drawn perpendicularly to the edge it is scraping.

Sharpening:

To sharpen the edge of a bone or wooden scraper, I use flint type stones that have been snapped in half to produce sharp squared edges. The squared edge doesn't crush like a flaked edge does. I've also used mussel shells, or the edge of any handy rock. They worked but not as quickly. Retouching the edge of a bone hide scraper takes about 20 seconds. I typically do this a few times per hide, using a sharp flint flake to scrape alongside the edge. Novices may need to resharpen multiple times per hide, because they take more strokes to do the same job. After a few hides you may need to rework the bevel (this is the general area that narrows into the actual edge).

Wear patterns:

After scraping a few hides, and sharpening your tool several times, the working edge will usually become curved. This increases your tool to beam contact area (see p. 60), which makes scraping more difficult. Once you start to get the curved wear pattern, it will reinforce itself. As you work, the pressure on the scraper will cause it to slide into the lowest spot, which is the center of the curve, reinforcing the wear pattern. To avoid this, try to equally use and sharpen the entire working edge. Once the curve becomes pronounced, sit down and spend some time getting it flat again.

Some Recommendations

I've scraped about two dozen deer hides primitively. The first half dozen I scraped with their own unmodified ulna-radii. Now, I wouldn't use one except in a pinch. Their natural edge is convenient, but their natural curve is not. You need to use a really narrow beam to get a decent bite. This slows down scraping considerably. Rib bones are also naturally curved. However, the way that you need to hold them prevents the problem that ulna-radii have. Instead, the curve forces you to hold your hands awkwardly. A good solution is to straighten the rib bone by soaking and heating. For a longer term scraper, I recommend modified cannon bones, straightened ribs, or wood with a bone insert. These tools are comfortable to hold and have straight working edges. Experiment with hard woods and hafted stone scrapers.

Wringing

Wringing is done the exact same way as described in *The Basic Method*. You can easily substitute a smooth living tree branch for the horizontal pole that is described.

Braining

Anything that can hold a gallon of liquid can be used as a braining container. Some ideas include: rawhide, bark containers, pottery, watertight baskets, wooden troughs, rock mortars, the deer's own stomach, or even just depressions in bedrock.

Place the brains in the container with a small amount of water and hand mash the brains to a paste. Next, you should heat some rocks and then place them in the container (pottery can be heated directly on the fire). Select rocks that are the size of an egg, have no obvious fissures and that aren't from wet areas (these can explode from the pressure of water escaping). Heat them in the fire. When they are glowing hot, use stick tongs to place them in the braining container. Blow off any ash first. Stir them around in the container to avoid burning the sides. It should not take more than a few to quickly bring a half gallon of liquid up to the hot bath temperature.

You can also simply paste the brains onto the hide. This allows you to get by with a much smaller container. It needs to be big enough to mix brains with a cup of water but no bigger. Mash the brains and water into a wet paste consistency. Lay your hide out on the ground so that the center is in a shallow depression. Put in the brain solution, adding more water until there is at least a quart. Then smear the solution all over the hide. Bring the edges into the wet trough and get them brained. Keep manipulating the hide until it's thoroughly saturated. Remember anywhere that doesn't soak up fully, won't come out soft.

Don't smear pure brains into the hide. I have had some penetration problems that were clearly the result of doing this. Wherever we had smeared just brains did not come out soft, whereas everything else did. These stiff areas were in very atypical regions and followed the pattern of smearing precisely. Perhaps the smeared brains created their own barrier, preventing oils from penetrating further. This happened to four hides in a row before we figured out the problem.

Brain Additives and Substitutes

In an actual primitive situation it is very important to conserve your brains. If for some reason your hide does not soften the first time, you will need some back up. If possible catch the brain dressing as it is wrung out of the hide. If you find yourself short on brains, try one of these additives or substitutes employed by Native American tribes.

Substitutes. Instead of brains, tribes of the southern Colorado River region used saguaro cactus seeds. The Tonto Apache used jojoba berries, a plant renowned for its emulsified oils. Sometimes tribes in the southeast substituted mashed sweetcorn. Peoples from the Gulf of Georgia used fish and sea mammal oils, with a somewhat different methodology. They would completely saturate the skin repeatedly with oils and then they'd degrease it with urine. This would chemically create a different type of leather, known as oil-tan. This is paralleled in modern days by the tanneries that use cod oil to saturate the skin and then degrease it with sodium carbonate, resulting in what is popularly known as chamois.

Additives. Other substances were put directly into the soak solution with the brains. Some of these added oils, possibly to improve the *feel* of the finished skin, or at the least to help the brains go farther. Other additives may have improved penetration by disrupting mucus bonds. Here are some common additives:

      Oils: spinal fluid, liver, bone marrow, tallows and fats, fish
            oils, acorn soup, pine nuts, corn meal
      Soaps: soaproot lather (amole lily), yucca, wood ashes
      (creates soap when mixed with oil.
      Tannins: decayed wood (mostly fir), wild rhubarb.
      Decomposition: The Sanpoil, Thompson, Wishram and
Okanogan purposely decomposed brains for months before using. What this added, besides stench, I do not know, but I imagine something. *Would you try this out?* And then tell me all about it.

Sewing Holes

I have never figured out a way to sew holes primitively as well as I can with modern needles. There just isn't any material from which one can make small to moderately sized needles with sharp points. I have sewn several holes at this pre-softening stage with a bone awl and sinew thread. This was quite slow for me and the awl holes came out fairly large when the hide was softened, though not too outrageous. One trick that could work is to sew the holes when the hide is already softened and then leave the hide out in some moist night air. You can then give the hide a quick reworking. The moisture will allow the fibers to realign around the holes, so that they lie flat. This way the awl holes won't stretch out nearly so much. Even better would be to think of a way to lightly steam just the area around the holes, so that you don't have to deal with the rest of the hide. Probably the most practical way to deal with holes is simply to patch them after smoking. The pre-metal Native American garments I have looked at in museums were done this way.

Softening

Softening primitively is pretty straightforward. **For hand softening** just be sure that you have at least one abrading tool. Its really helpful, though not necessary, to have a staking post and a cable type tool too. If you don't, be extra on top of stretching your hide, so that it never reaches a point of tightness that only a cable can bring it back from.

For frame softening, the frame can be lashed together with thick rawhide thongs. Use a large bone awl for making good-sized holes in the edge of the hide. Hang the hide up with buckskin, rawhide or plant fiber cordage. I frequently use thongs that have been cut from stiff edges. For tools use the stake described in *The Basic Method* and one of the abrading tools.

Tools

Tools can make softening easier. They are particularly good at working an area intensively. If you forget to work an area for a spell, the glues begin to set and fibers start to lock to one another. Sometimes they will lock harder than hand stretching can easily undo. Tools can concentrate force and break up those bonds, loosening the area back up. At the very least, you need one tool that will abrade. This can be as simple as a shell or broken rock.

Abraders

These tools are especially effective abraders and not very useful for stretching.

* **Pumice** is excellent. It is described in the *Tools You Will Need* chapter.

* **Bone sponge** is also a very effective abrader. There is abrasive sponge tissue in nearly every bone, but the largest and most useful piece is from the ball of the humerus. The sponge of fresh bone is often soaked in marrow, so use bones that have aged a bit. Buffalo bone sponge was commonly used by the Plains Indians.

* **Other** possible abraders include sandstone and shark skin.

Softening tools counter clockwise from upper left (with notes on pre-contact Native American use):

__Pumice__, great for abrading without overly roughing up surface, extensive distribution. __Mussel shells__ abrade and stretch. Used as found, convenient thumb slot, and very effective. Common tool on west coast.

Simple and retouched __flint flakes, and slate shards__. Many types of stone used including split river rocks {skipping stone types}, extensive distribution.

__Stone and wood elbow adze__, used with frame. Abrades and stretches. Used by buffalo hunting tribes.

__Hafted knapped stone__, abrades and stretches. Plateau, Tlingit, Ojibwa, Natchez.

__Buffalo humerus core__, from bulbous end of bone. It is porous and very abrasive, after aging. Plains.

__Elk antler__, beveled. Abrades and stretches. Plateau, NW California.

__Cannon bone__, beveled. Abrades and stretches. California, Plateau, Apache.

__Deer antler__, beveled. Abrades and stretches. Also, any thing abrasive or with an edge: turtle shells, sandstone, buffalo tongues!

Hand Held Stretching Tools

The hide needs to be held taut to use these tools. Hanging the hide from buckskin thongs is an easy way to go about this.

Shells make excellent stretching and abrading tools. Hold them in your hand, with your thumb placed inside the hollow. Drag and scrape the sharp edge into and over the hide. Shells are great because they come totally ready to use, and you can make a feast out of the contents. Some shells to try include mussel, clam and turtle. I really like and frequently use mussel shells.

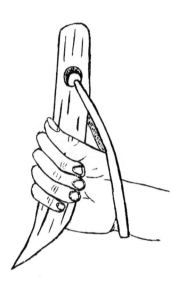

Beveled antler, bones or wood, make excellent stretching tools and pretty good abraders when the edge is sharp. Your wrist will get less tired if you put a thong through the back end of the tool and slide your hand through this, using it as a brace. Their size allows you to use a lot of force. Modern versions include any beveled plastic or metal pipe.

Stones can be broken to create a sharp edge. They make effective abraders and stretchers. Make sure the edge is smooth rather than jagged and not too sharp. These kinds of tools are extremely common at archaeological sites. Try any of the flints, slate or simply find a good skipping stone and split it in half.

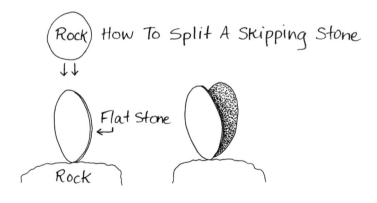

Stretching Tools

"**Cables**" All of these alternatives are just as effective as stretching tools but not as durably abrasive as the aircraft cable.

Cables from left to right:

Braided rawhide (buffalo sinew also used). Both mentioned mostly in connection with tanning buffalo robes. Stretches hide well, a little abrasion, but not very durable (note wear in center). I might try a rawhide thong next time, for same effect, and no time braiding.

Buffalo scapula, center of bone removed, working edge beveled sharp. Stretches and abrades, durable. Really shreds!

Wild grape vine, lasts longer if used while still living. Some initial abrasion, good stretching. Also, any rough barked woody sapling, vine, or branch. Comanche, Potawatomi, northern California, eastern Great Basin.

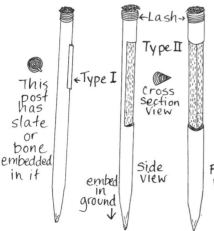

This post has slate or bone embedded in it

←Type I

←Lash→

Type II

Cross section View

Side View

embed in ground ↓

Front view

I really like these beveled wood "cables". They are the most durable of the lot and very abrasive when the edge is sharp. However they do need to be sharpened frequently. What I want to try next is embedding a piece of slate or other appropriate stones in the wood and working the hide across it.

Staking posts are excellent stretching tools and can have stone implanted in their tips to make them better abraders. They really help you put your weight into the stretching. These tools are also the best for opening up damped back hides (see staking posts p. 153 and see damping back p. 149).

Two staking posts are left of center. The one on the left has a piece of chert embedded in the top. This makes the tool more abrasive. The hide in back is hanging from buckskin thongs. We use this set-up to work the hide with various hand-tools. The hide frame is lashed together with rawhide. The hide is tied on to it with half-tanned buckskin. Framed hides are easily worked with a wooden stake or a wooden stake with a stone

Making a Smoking Sack

Use obsidian or other sharp rocks to trim stiff edges. Trim everything that is stiff except for what will be the open end of the sack. This will be in contact with the ground. Leave these edges there so that they can get dirty instead of the buckskin. Use hide glue to make the sack. To apply the glue I use a feather paint brush, and a clam shell pot. The clam shell pot is only so-so.

A soapstone or ceramic pot would help maintain the more even temperature that hide-glue appreciates.

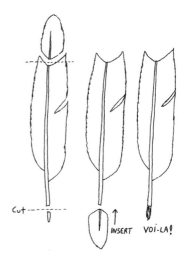

Feathers make simple and effective glue applicators. Also try chewed twig tips, tied bundles of deer hair, dried grass, or your good old finger.

Smoking

Don't bother with a smoking skirt. Instead, use the same setup as described in *The Basic Method* and pin the neck to the ground with rocks, earth or stakes. There are basically two approaches to primitive smoking: to make a sack that you funnel smoke into, or a frame

that you drape the hide over. I've done both, though the second method only a few times. The frame method looks easier, but isn't. There is way more draft, loss of smoke and opportunity for flare-up. Wherever the frame contacts the hide doesn't smoke, so you need to move the hide around regularly. It just takes longer to get the hide smoked! The only time I would do it would be in a survival situation where I did not want to take the time to make glue, and would settle for a so-so smoking job.

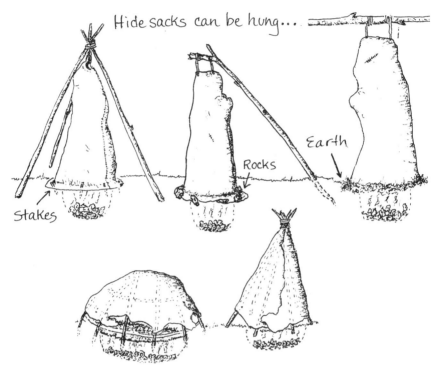

Hide sacks can be hung...

Stakes

Rocks

Earth

.... or hides can be draped over a frame

Buckskin was made for many thousands of years using tools of wood, bone, stone and shell. By learning how to tan with these tools, you will make some trusted friends ready for many applications. Need a spoon for the ice cream? Grab a mussel shell. Forgot your knife? Maybe a split rock would do the trick. The surrounding world just keeps looking friendlier and friendlier.

As it is, a beginner can learn to tan a hide quite nicely using nature's tools. Imagine if you had spent your whole lifetime tanning thirty hides a year primitively. And imagine that you are learning from grandma or grandpa who are passing on many generations worth of honing a *really* efficient method. Maybe primitive people didn't have it so bad. Maybe they had plenty of time to go swimming and chase their lovers through the tall grass. Maybe they just hung out making silly deer fart jokes.

Hide Glue

You can make your own glue from the pieces of hide that stick out so wildly from the main body that it doesn't seem worth the effort to tan them. These rough edges or particularly holey sections are not worth much in the finished buckskin, and create a lot of extra work. So you might as well make some glue.

Extraneous edges can be used for glue

Hide glue is extremely strong and bonds excellently with hides, wood and natural fibers. It does not bond with metals or plastics. Glue is made from the collagen fibers of the skin, the same fibers that are the basis of buckskin, as well as hooves, bones, and sinew. Skins are prepared for glue in the same way as they are for buckskin, by clearing away everything but the collagen fibers.

How to

After the 'rinsing and neutralization' step of the basic method, cut off any of those extraneous edge protrusions and dry. It is important that the scraps dry completely before making the glue. The proteins go through some transformation that is crucial to the glue making process. When you have collected a quantity, you are ready to make your glue. Soak the dry scraps overnight in just enough water to cover. The next day, heat on a very low heat, approximately 150 degrees, for four to eight hours (the longer it steeps the more glue is extracted, but it gets slightly weaker. Many people pour off a first

Dried hide scraps ready for glue making

pouring after four hours and then put in fresh water and make another batch). This heat should be too hot for your hands but not hot enough to make steam or bubbles. Keep a lid on the pot so that no water evaporates. Use a spoon to skim off any scuzz that collects on the surface as it cooks. Pour off, straining out the solid through an old t-shirt or cheese cloth. Hide glue is water soluble and will wash out of anything.

This poured off glue will rot very quickly, so you must make all efforts to do the following steps in a timely fashion. Allow to cool over night. By morning it should have jelled and look like jello. Which in fact, it is (Yes, many

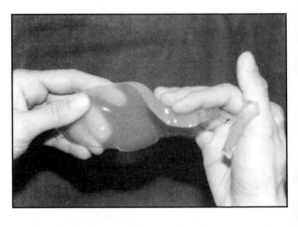

of us spent our childhoods joyfully slurping flavored and sweetened hide glue). This is a good time to play with it.

Then slice into very thin wafers, as thin as you can, and dry in a drafty but cool location. If it is too warm at this point it will liquefy and make a mess. When the wafers become slightly leathery they can be moved to a warmer locale. Dry completely. The pieces will feel elastically brittle. Store.

To use, soak pieces in enough water to cover. Heat up to 150 degrees or so, but do not allow to boil, or even get close. If necessary dilute until syrup consistency. Hide glue works best if applied at 120 degrees. Ideal containers for heating and using hide glues are ones that heat up and cool down slowly. Ceramic and stone containers are two excellent tainers are two excellent

glue drying on screen

examples. Use these if you have them. If you don't, anything will do. You will need some setup to maintain this temperature steadily. The corner of a woodstove, or the hot ashes of an outdoor fire can offer a moderate enduring temperature. Set yourself up comfortably by one of these heat-sources, so that your glue-pot is on the heat while you glue. Hide glue can be applied with a paint brush. It is water soluble and easily cleaned up after.

Always maintain moderate temperatures when making and using hide glues. Do not allow to boil, or even come close to it. If your glue does get too hot, it is still usable, just weaker.

Other options. You can also use whole or parts of hides specially set aside for glue. Process as you would for buckskin through the end of the rinsing step, except don't bother removing the grain layer. Its a good use for hides that are so knifed up you wouldn't even consider tanning them.

You can use raw hair-on hides (you must dry them first), and it will yield a workable glue for many projects, but it is not nearly as strong as glue prepared in the above manner. Soaking the hide in lye or lime to clean out the interior, and scraping away the exterior layers of flesh, hair and epidermis, yields the strongest glue because it contains the least impurities. Clearness, lightness of color and smell are all signs of better glues. Using home made hide glue to glue hide sacks together is a good test of the quality. Good hide glue will work quite easily, while poor hide glue is totally frustrating.

Fortunately, hide glue is water soluble.

Rawhide

Rawhide is easily made using *The Basic Method* with these modifications:

* Flesh normally.
* Allow the hide to soak in the buck until the hair is falling out, and I mean falling. There is a stage where the hair can be pulled out fairly easily, but you want to be able to push it out simply by running your fingers over the surface.
* Instead of graining, just push the remaining hair off of the hide with your scraping tool or better, rub it off with a rag. Use as little pressure as possible, so that you don't remove any grain.
* Rinse before membraning so that the grain has tightened back down and won't get marred by the membraning. Also a towel can be placed over the beam at this point to protect the grain.
* Membrane as usual.

That's it! It can be dried flat and off-white by stretching it tightly in a frame, pegged to the ground or tacked to a piece of plywood. Drying it fully stretched taut, gives it that pleasing off-white color. If you want this, never give the rawhide a chance to contract as it dries. Tie the hide up into a frame as instructed in the frame softening section of *The Basic Method*, or tack it out on a piece of plywood. The frame must be stable and sturdy as the drying rawhide will torque and twist loosely constructed frames. Place your slits four inches apart so that there is even tension everywhere. Tie it up fairly tight. Dry slowly in a shady and cool spot. If the hide dries quickly it is more apt to warp the frame or to rip out its tie loops.

Making Stuff

Before making anything from your buckskin, soak it in a bucket of water, hand-wring, and lay it out completely flat to dry. All of that pulling, poking and stretching that your deerskin underwent during the softening process, influenced the shape that it dried in. By re-wetting the already soft and smoked skin, you allow it to settle into its true shape. Your finished clothing will be far less likely to shrink or expand when you wash it later — which will frequently happen otherwise. This applies to hand stretched as well as frame stretched skins. With wavy-edged hides, this rinsing and laying flat, will greatly decrease the waviness, making it easier to lay out a pattern. Rinsing will also get rid of the intensity of the smoke smell, which can be overwhelming, and reduce it to a pleasant campfire aroma.

When dry, hand stretch the skin to its original softness and abrade the membrane side to buff the surface texture. You can also lightly pumice the surface of the grain side to soften the surface, but it might unevenly scuff away some of the smoke color, leaving marks. Do what you feel is necessary to make it feel really good. Don't overdo the stretching or the edges may become wavy again.

Clothing Styles and Concepts

There are ways to take advantage of the different qualities of buckskin, and methods of garment design, to create the garment that you desire. The first major decision to make is what style of garment you wish to make. You can create anything, from a hide simply wrapped around your waist and pinned in place, to a highly tailored jacket.

There is no reason to be limited by any traditional styles of clothing. We like to mix modern and primitive design. An example of this would be a fitted jacket with the bottom edge left raw in the shape of the deer skin. That way I get the fitted jacket that I want but maintain some of the form and spirit of the hide. Here is a good reminder from Captain Jim Riggs, *"Blue Mountain Buckskin"*:

> *"Nobody says you have to conform to any past or present standards in the type and style of clothing you make and wear. You (and the deer) created the buckskin — now, create a way to wear it!"*

Primitive and Freeform

This type of clothing maintains the essential form and spirit of the deerskin and can be very beautiful. It is also a very simple way to make functional, comfortable clothing. With the minimum of cutting and sewing, simply attach the hides to one another so that they make some kind of body covering. Take advantage of the natural shapes of the deerskin. The stitching can be very simple and sparse. Buckskin is strong stuff and it doesn't take much to hold it together. Here are some samples of a **primitive style**:

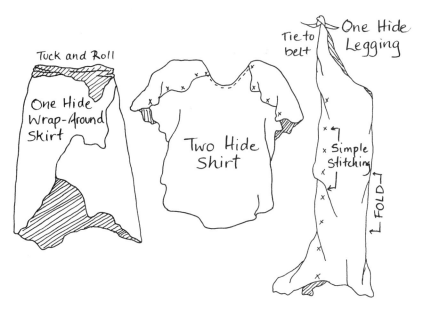

Form fitting and Tailored

Tailoring is an art unto itself. If it's your first time, I highly encourage you to buy a pattern or make one from something that fits you well. Take it apart along the seams and follow the pattern strictly. It is tempting to take different parts from our favorite clothes and create our ideal shirt or pants. It is *really* easy to screw this up, losing some crucial detail of the curve of the body. The pattern pieces of a fitted garment are usually shapes that you would never logically think of on your own. They work really well, because tailors have spent a lot of time figuring them out.

I used to be casual and adventurous in my tailoring. Over time, I have found that I really like clothes that fit well, not just sort of. Your buckskin clothes will last a very long time, so take the time to make them well. It often takes just as long to make and lay out patterns as it does to assemble them into clothing.

Michelle Richards' classic buckskin jacket

Dew-Claw bags
by Michelle Richards
These beautiful dew-claw bags are made by drying the lower leg skins of a deer or elk out flat and untanned.

Beaded Pouch
by Michelle Richards
Beadworkers prefer to work on traditionally tanned hides because they are so much easier to put a needle through. Old Indian ladies who buy buckskin from us, test them by poking their beading needles in and out.

Buckskin Hunting Coat
by Ken Smith.
"Coat is cut so I can swing an ax, or shoulder a rifle with no binding and will still fit 2 heavy shirts underneath."

Painting on brain tan
Lee Secrest uses earth pigments and sharpened sticks to paint intricate designs on his brain tanned deer, elk, antelope and bighorn hides. His work is exhibited all over the world, even the Smithsonian.

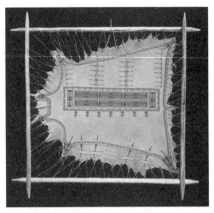

Métis Jacket
The Métis tradition of beautifully tailored buckskin coats goes back to the 1700's. The Métis were mixed-blood French and Indians from the Canadian side of the Great Lakes. The buffalo and floral motifs are done in beadwork.

Buckskin Dress
by Michelle Richards
Michelle's modern style dress has a yoke made from dark smoked buckskin and no fringe.

The Blankenship kids:
*Tyree, Tikla, and Teale
with braintanned
'Coon' skin caps.*

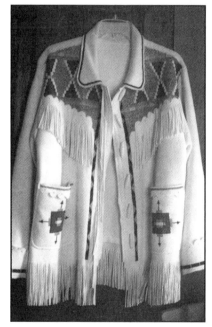

'New West' Jacket
*by Robin Moore
Robin made this gorgeous jacket
out of white, unsmoked brain
tanned hides.*

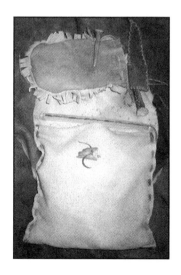

Pouches and Sheath
*by Vaughn Terpack
Pouches, knife sheaths and the like are good
projects to start with. Notice the way Vaughn
used buckskin of contrasting colors to show off
the fancy stitching on his knife sheath. He also
sewed in a piece of wood to stiffen the opening
of his large pouch.*

Ron Macy: tanner, flintknapper, falconer & hunk.

Bighorn Sheepskin Dress
by Nancy Fonicello
Because of their thinness, Bighorn
Sheep skins were considered one of
the choice materials to make dresses
from on the northern Plains. They
are extremely rare and hard to get
nowadays (because the animals are
rare and hard to get).

Sunny & Prairie Rose *tan, travel*
and craft, living out of a 'gypsy
wagon' built on the back of an old
Model T truck.

Brain-tanned Buffalo Hide Tipi
by Wes Housler
*Most folks don't realize that tipis
were tanned soft (the ultimate
braintanners' project). This
fourteen foot tipi is composed of
numerous hides stitched together
with Buffalo backstrap sinew.*

**Indian Artifact Reproductions and
Restorations**
by Ric Carter & Danneil Juhl
*"I did all the tanning, the
construction, and bead work on all the
items. We firmly believe in shoot 'em,
skin 'em, eat 'em, tan 'em, and wear
'em!*

Abo Adventurers
*With years of practice
and eating right, you too
could look like this!
From left to right: (top
row) Mike Clinchy, Peg
Mathewson, Kole Riggs,
Matt Richards, Walt &
Jim Riggs. (bottom row)
Jeff 'Roadkill' Damm,
John Mein, Ron Macy
& Michelle Riley*

Tailored Jacket

Simpl Vest

2 Hide Skirt

3 Hide Dress

3 Hide Shirt

Seasonal Considerations

Hot Weather Clothes

Buckskin is porous, allowing your skin to breathe and preventing that clammy feeling that other leathers have. However this same porous quality makes buckskin insulative, storing some of your body heat in the spaces between the fibers. To make cool summer clothes while still protecting your skin from brush, sun and nudity laws, use very thin hides (does and young bucks) and sew airy open seams, especially by the armpits and along the sides of the torso. See types of open seams p. 206...and decorative holes p. 220.

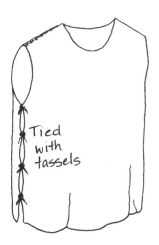
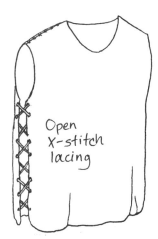

Cold Weather Clothes

Use thicker skins and sew tight seams. Make your clothing loose but tailored to your body, to trap your body heat. Buckskin is very insulative and if you can create garments that hold that warmth in, it will keep you quite warm. Also, because of its tight weave, it cuts the wind as well as anything I've ever worn. As with any clothing, two moderate layers are more insulative than one super thick layer.

Wet Weather Clothes

Wear something water resistant over your skins. Buckskin will soak-in water like cotton. In the old days people wore wool over their buckskin, and in the really old days, shredded bark, grass ponchos, or furs (or they took their buckskins off and enjoyed the rain on their own skin). Don't fight your buckskins trying to make them fit into the role of rain-gear; they can't do everything.

Native American Solutions

Amongst Native American tribes there was a very clear pattern of garment styles: very simple unformed clothing in the warmest climes, usually just hides wrapped around and held in place by a thong or button, progressing to highly tailored form fitting clothing brought to its logical extreme by the Inuit and Eskimo. In the climates in between were peoples such as the plains and woodlands Indians who had simple, loose fitting shirts and leggings.

Pants, Breeches And Leggings

The durability of buckskin is particularly well suited to garments that cover your legs. In the course of time, three different styles of buckskin leg-wear have evolved, each with its own unique qualities.

Leggings

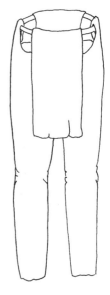

Leggings are just what the word sounds like, coverings for the legs. They cover the legs but not the crotch or buttocks. These were typically covered by a breechcloth. This was the common style of many Native American peoples. The advantages of leggings and a breechcloth are that they offer protection to the legs and groin, but allow complete freedom of leg movement and ventilation. In colder weather a long shirt that reaches down to the mid-thigh is worn.

Leggings were one of the first items I made out of buckskin. The complete freedom of movement that they allowed was striking. The draftiness in cold weather took some getting used to, but not much.

To make leggings, simply wrap an appropriately sized hide around each leg, stitch in place with plenty of room and ideally leave a flap that can be looped or tied over a waist belt. Otherwise, sew one in. The seam should be down the outside of the leg. Your waist-belt should be fairly wide so that it does not dig in.

Breeches

I recently made some pants and unintentionally discovered breeches. I put a gusset in the crotch, because I regularly rip out this seam in the activity of
my life. I made them a bit short because I notice
that I always role up my pant legs so they won't get
wet. I roll these up anyway, and thus they turned
into breeches. And I love them!

Breeches were the European and American colonists' answer to buckskin leg-wear. Breeches are similar to pants, except that they have a much roomier
crotch and seat, and they only extend down the leg to the upper shins. The baggy seat creates the freedom of movement of leggings, with the insulation of pants. The shorter leg length keeps absorbent buckskin out of the wet grass. Shins were bare or covered with wool socks to repel the wetness of fields and forest, while buckskin pro-tected the knees, thighs and seat. You can find patterns for breeches anywhere that carries old-style patterns.

Pants

Wearing buckskin pants is similar to wearing old jeans. If you are comfortable in old jeans then you will love buckskin pants. First find a pair of pants that fit you well. Rip the seams open and use them as the pattern. Then add a quarter inch seam allowance to each seam as buckskin seams require more material than machine stitched pants. Err on the loose side of things as you can always make them snugger. Most people err on the tight side, which is harder to fix.

A buckskin waistband *will* stretch out and loosen if not reinforced with a hem and stitching. For this reason a drawstring waist is simpler to get right than a buttoned one. If you make a buttoned waist, make it a little snug and it will loosen.

Moccasins

Buckskin was the original material for moccasins, and they were semi-disposable. Moose is by far the most durable, and because of its thickness, they are the most comfortable. People assume that Elk would be excellent because of its thickness, but its loose fiber structure causes it to wear out faster than thinner deer hide mocs. Where Moose wasn't historically available, moccasins were quickly made and quickly worn out. Because buckskin fibers are exposed and separated from one another, they abrade and wear down relatively quickly when used for footwear. What retails for "moccasins" in modern times would have been called a shoe in the old days, because it has the slick grain layer still on it.

In colonial and pioneer America there were two basic types of footwear, shoes made from bark-tanned leather and moccasins of buckskin. The shoes were worn in towns and on streets, while moccasins were worn in the woods. The bark-tan shoes of the time were stiff and so slick soled you could ski down a grassy hill in them.

> "Walking through the woods (in street shoes) is not like traveling on a well-beaten road. In the former your progress is often necessarily slow and laborious on account of having to force your way through rank grass and many creeping vines....Moreover the soles of your shoes soon become as slick as glass by rubbing on dry leaves and grass, so that you are frequently slipping backward instead of going forward." *John Duvall, under the heading 'Moccasins vs. Shoes'.*

Rubber changed the world of shoes to a degree that those of us raised on it can not really imagine. It bridged the gap between comfortable and durable. Compared to rubber, deerskin soles wear out so fast it's ridiculous. The Indian and pioneer way was to go barefoot *most* of the time and wear moccasins for travel and hunting, carrying spares along the way. They didn't *need* footwear, because their feet were tough. Those fancy Indian moccasins you see in books were just that, their fancy ones. They didn't wear those around, because they would wear out, wasting all of that decorative work.

I'm telling you all of this so that you won't have any false expectations. Deerskin moccasins *are* extremely comfortable. For those with semi-tough feet, they offer enough protection to be able to travel fast and not look at the rocks and sticks you are stepping on. You feel much more connected to the earth as you walk. They are undoubtedly much better for your feet and posture.

If you are going to wear them as a daily footwear avoid wearing them on cement and asphalt, and they will last a lot longer. Do not wear them in wet conditions. They just get sloppy, and the endless wet to dry process is hard on them. If you have an opportunity to get brain-tan moose, they will make more durable moccasins.

Moccasins *are* easy to make. I can make a simple pair in a few hours with all primitive tools. If you want to make elaborate moccasins for occasional wear, go for it! They are beautiful and comfortable. A moccasin book with patterns for many tribes is: *"Craft Manual of North American Indian Footwear,"* by George White. It can be a bit confusing to use, but it will give you a lot of ideas. There is a good side-seam moccasin pattern in Jim Riggs' *"Blue Mountain Buckskin"*.

Simple Tailoring Tips

Making Patterns From Other Clothes

This is easy to do. Find a piece of clothing that you want to replicate out of buckskin. If you don't have what you want at home, go to a thrift store and buy one for a few dollars. Choose something that fits you fairly loosely. Open up the seams, and take it completely apart. Do not try to make patterns from clothing that you haven't taken apart. There are usually subtleties of form that you will miss. Trace out each pattern piece on cardboard or stiff paper. Be accurate.

Creating New Patterns

Though time consuming, creating new patterns can be very satisfying. You can make exactly the garment that you envision. Find clothes that contain parts of what you want to make, and make patterns from them. Mix and match, using your imagination to fill in the gaps, or figure out exactly how they should fit together. *Always* make a practice garment out of an old sheet, first. This way you make your mistakes and learn on your sheet instead of on your buckskin. Get it completely right before moving on to buckskin. Don't leave any room for surprises.

Shaping To Fit The Body's Contours

In fitting the contours of one's shape, lines no longer fall straight but rather are curved, cut, extended, or angled. Here are some traditional techniques to help shape garments to the unique forms and angles of the human body.

Contoured Seams: Seams curve outward to accommodate the fullest parts of the body and inward to conform to the thinner parts.

Darts: Darts create curves within the main body of the fabric to give space for the breasts and butt. They are triangular cuts that start at the edge of a seam and come to a point within the curve that is being created. The two new raw edges are then sewn together. The point of the cut should always fall short of the center of the protrusion. Darts will change the alignment of the seam edge and need to be accounted for in the pattern rather than after the seam has been cut. Please refer to a basic sewing and tailoring book for a better understanding of just where to place and how to compensate for darts. A good one is: Reader's Digest *Complete Guide to Sewing*, Pleasantville, NY 1985

Gussets: Gussets are triangular or diamond shaped pieces of material that are added into armpit and crotch seams. They add material to the area creating greater freedom of movement and looseness. Gussets are generally added into armpits as a fix-it technique when they are too tight. With crotch seams they are often part of the pattern, allowing for freer leg movement and keeping seams off of sensitive organs.

Basic Shoulder Fitting.

Shoulders come in many shapes and sizes. No two are alike but all have similarities. When fitting a garment to your upper body, consider these two aspects of the human form:

(1) The distance from the armpit to the midpoint of the shoulder is always greater up the back than up the chest. You must allow for this difference in any garment that has a shoulder seam. The back is generally an inch or more longer from the armpit to the shoulder seam.

If you do not account for this bodily form in your garment design, your body will force it upon you. Your shoulder seam will slide backwards pulling the front of your garment up with it and out of alignment. Your neckline will be pulled up to your neck in front and fall off of it in back. This can be very annoying. I did not know any of this when I made my first four shirts and they all had this problem. It's a real bummer to be strangled by your neckline after you've spent many hours tanning and constructing a buckskin shirt.

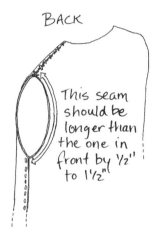

BACK

This seam should be longer than the one in front by ½" to 1½"

(2) The line along your shoulders drops and curves forward from the neck to the top of the arm. This applies to everyone no matter how good their posture. Most patterns will account for this shape by cutting the shoulder line at an angle, but with the front piece's angle less steep. This is a finer fitting technique so don't worry about

The Sane Tailor's Warning: If you are creating your own patterns or altering someone else's, always make a mock-up with an old sheet, *before* making any cuts.

it too much.

Lay Out

The Lay of the Hide and Why It's Important

Because our material was once the skin of a living deer, it varies in thickness and stretch from one section to another. These differences are logical if you think about the function of different parts of the body and skin.

The **stomach** shrinks and enlarges through the course of every day, and is in a protected part of the body. As a result your buckskin that was once the covering of the belly is thin and very stretchy in all directions.

The **backbone** only experiences mild degrees of movement and is in a very exposed part of the body that is important to protect. This part of a finished hide is not very stretchy and is one of the thicker areas.

The **neck** is a very vulnerable area. The huge arteries and veins of the neck are not protected by bones, and they are the preferred target of mountain lions, the deer's number one predator. This part of the finished skin is very thick.

It is good to understand these differences when constructing garments. Most clothing items are laid out so that the backbone runs the length of the piece. The backbone's unwillingness to stretch much adds stability to the shape. For example a pant leg is laid out so that the backbone runs from the waist to the ankle, preventing it from stretching or shrinking much. If you laid out your pant leg, belly to belly, the shape changing potentials of the

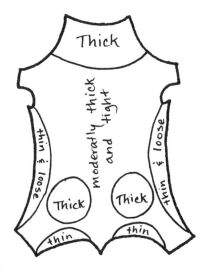

belly could really alter things later.

If you do not have a lot of tanned skins you may want to fit all of your pattern pieces into as few hides as possible. You will probably get away with this, but try to follow the backbone as much as you can and don't lay out any clothing parts on a diagonal. This invites uneven stretching and twisting.

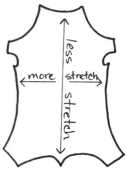

The other quality to consider is thickness. Lay out your patterns to take advantage of thick and thin spots. Use thick spots for moccasins, bags or parts of your garment that experience the most wear. Place thin spots where their thin, soft, flexibility will be appreciated.

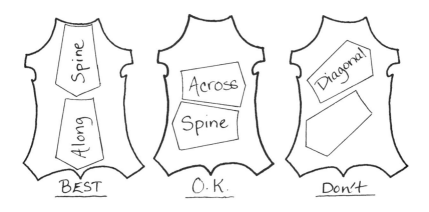

Laying Out Patterns On Hides

Place pattern pieces on the flesh side of the hide. Arrange and rearrange until you find the best location for each. Use "the lay of the hide" section to make good lay out decisions. Trace the pattern with a pencil or charcoal, it will come off. Before you start to cut, be absolutely sure that you have layed out all of the pattern pieces correctly. Have you accidently made two right sleeves?

Working With Buckskin

Buckskin is different than any other material. It has its very own ways and behaviors. Understanding these ways will help you to make quality, fitted and lasting clothing. The difference between working with buckskin and fabric can be summed up in one sentence: *Buckskin will not unravel, but it does stretch, and can thus change its shape.*

Because it won't unravel: There is no need to worry about hems, or double stitched seams, or making lots of tiny little stitches. All you need are big easy stitches. For these reasons it is easy for anyone to make a buckskin garment, regardless of their sewing experience.

Because it does stretch: You need to reinforce or hem any raw edge that you don't want to get stretched out and wavy. This is particularly important if you are making form-fitting clothing. If you are making very simple loose garments there is less stress on the raw edges which are then less likely to stretch. If they do it will show less.

A good example of how to approach this is demonstrated by a buttonhole. With fabric, you are trying to prevent unraveling so you use the buttonhole stitch. With buckskin unraveling is not an issue but stretch is, and if your buttonhole stretches bigger, your button will pop out. So you use the running or saddle stitch. By stitching parallel to the raw edge, you reinforce it, preventing stretch.

For Fabric

For Buckskin

Button Hole Stitch

Another example is a sleeve cuff. If the cuff is left as a raw edge it will stretch out.

Raw   Hemmed

(Inside of hide)

If the edge is folded under and stitched with a running stitch, then it will stay put.

Turned Hem To Prevent Stretch

Clothing Construction

Types of Tight Seams

Tight seams attach the pieces of buckskin snugly together. This is ideal for cool and cold weather clothing, bags, quivers, moccasins and more. There are three types:

Overlapping or Flat seams. This seam can be used just about anywhere. It will show the stitching and expose it to wear, so you should lace them together with buckskin thongs.

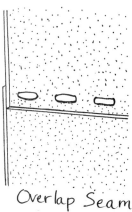

Overlap Seam

Hidden seams. This seam is used when you want to sew with sinew, though they can be laced together too. The stitching is more protected from wear and invisible on the outside. Do not use hidden seams where they will be pressed against the body, such as in a shoulder seam. I sew hidden seams with sinew, wherever I don't care to see lacing, or have its bulk. I lace hidden seams where strength and resistance to wear are crucial, as in moccasins, and certain bags.

Lace with the in-sides facing Out!

Hidden Seam

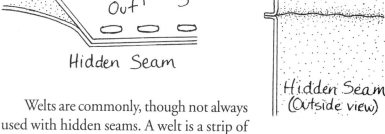

Hidden Seam (Outside view)

Welts are commonly, though not always used with hidden seams. A welt is a strip of buckskin that is sewn or laced in between the two main pieces. It adds extra assurance that the stitching will not show or experience wear. It can serve the same purpose while creating fringe (see fringe, p. 217). I especially use welts on moccasins and bags.

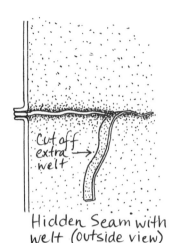

Cut off
extra →
welt

Hidden Seam with
welt (outside view)

To make a welt, cut a strip of buckskin a half inch wide for lacing and a quarter inch wide for sewing with sinew. This gives you assurance that you won't miss the welt when stitching. Cut it as long as the seam. When the seam is complete, trim welt to desired width. If making a fringed welt, stitch large scraps into the seam. Use scraps that are as long as you want your fringe to be. You can use one big scrap, or several small ones placed side by side.

Meeting seams. There are a few stitches that will bring your two pieces of buckskin together so that they just meet. The baseball stitch is commonly used to do this. It is excellent where low seam bulk is important, as on shoulders, where a bulky seam will dig in under the weight of a pack. See baseball stitch, p. 212.

Types of open seams

Open seams are great for warm weather buckskins. Here are a couple ways of creating open seams:

(1) Cinch the two pieces of buckskin together in several places with thong ties. These are known as tassels. The closer you make the tassels, the warmer your garment will be. See tassels, p. 219.

(2) Stitch a big open X-stitch. See X-stitch, p. 211.

Lacing and Sewing

You can either lace or sew your buckskins together. To lace you poke holes with an awl and pull buckskin lacing through with a dull big-eyed needle. To sew use a glover's needle, and real or artificial sinew.

Lacing is extremely strong and durable, as well as decorative. Sewing is faster to do, and creates a finer hidden seam, but is not quite as durable. I use both, depending on where the seam is, whether I want a flat or a hidden seam, how much stress it is going to undergo, and what I want it to look like. For example, I like to sew the seams of gloves, for a hidden seam with minimal bulk, but lace my shoulder seams together for a flat seam that is durable.

Lacing Seams

Buckskin lacing can be very simple or very complex and ornate. You can use thin thong and closely spaced holes or large thong and widely spaced holes. The type of
stitch you use will deter-
mine the length of lace and
pattern of holes. Functionally the simple **running
stitch** is all that you need. I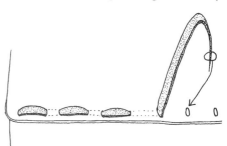
use it three fourths of the
time. It is plenty strong, and
can look elegant to brawny.

Making the thong. You can make thong from scraps or inten-tionally prepared circles. If you cut thong from stretchy thin areas it will stretch longer and thin out. Cut wide to compensate. From thicker tighter areas the thong will remain closer to the width that you cut it (see illustration of hide sections properties). Scars and stiff spots are weak and tend to break. Try to avoid them. Deal with it if you can't. After cutting thong stretch it well before using. The best is to wet it and stretch. This will keep your stitching from getting sloppy and loose later.

To prepare thong for lacing, taper the end that will go through the eye of the needle. Cut it as thin as will hold up. Have the taper run for a good inch or so. It will be doubled back as you lace and thinness will make it easy to pull through the holes. This is the key to lacing pleasure. In the end of the thong opposite the narrow tip, poke an awl hole. This hole will be used to lock the beginning of your lacing seam.

Get a big eyed, dull tipped needle or make one out of bone. You can find 'tapestry' needles at most fabric shops and they work quite well. Sharp tipped needles catch in the buckskin as you stitch, making it much more difficult.

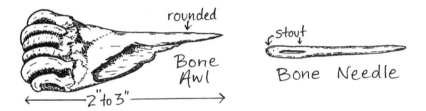

Preparing the seam. Poke holes with a very round awl. If its not round it will slice rather than open up a space in the skin. The slice creates a "tearing edge" that is only going to enlarge or rip out. If you want to use thin thong, poke holes closer together and not too big. Ideally you want to be able to pull the thong through, but have it feel snug as you pull, rather than super easy. Poke holes 1/4 inch to 1/3 inch from the edge. If you use bigger thong you can poke fewer and slightly bigger holes. Make sure that your holes are evenly spaced if you want the stitching pattern to be uniform. Poke all of the holes for a seam before you start, following the pattern of your chosen stitch. Practice on a scrap first, to see what it will look like.

With a metal awl, you can place a softwood board under the seam you are poking and push right into the wood. Using a soft wood will save your awl, wrist and forearm. This can be very fast and helps keep your edges from stretching unevenly. You usually will need to go back through and enlarge the holes with your awl.

Don't use a wooden backing with a bone awl. It will crush the tip. Instead, simply hold the pieces in your hand and push the awl through. I usually push all the holes in one piece, and then go back, and using the first piece as a pattern, push through the holes I've already made into the second. The problem you can have is with the second piece stretching out by being pulled on. If this happens you will get to the end of your seam and still have three inches left on your second piece. This is a real bummer. To prevent this poke four or five sets of holes on both pieces, at different junctures along the seam, and tie them in place. Concentrate on making your holes meet up correctly when you get to each tied spot. An alternative is to glue the seam together with a thin line of hide glue, before you even start poking. The hide glue will hold everything in perfect alignment and easily wash out later. We've gotten more interested in using hide glue for this purpose, as it makes aligning the pieces really easy. And you know if its all going to work out before you ever punch a hole.

Stitching:

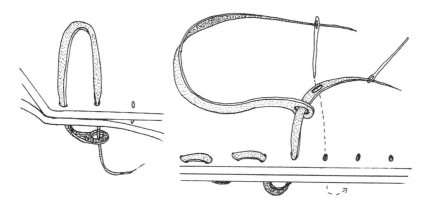

To Start: *From the inside of your future garment, push the needle up through the first two awl holes of one edge. Then go back down through the next pair of holes and the hole in the end of your thong. Pull snug.*

To splice a broken or short lace: *Just before the taper on the thong you are working with, poke an awl hole, just like you did on the back end, when you started. Make another thong the appropriate length. Poke an awl hole in the back end of this one. Lace the first thong through the hole in the second thong. Pull through until the hole in the first thong comes through. Next, lace the front end of the second thong through the hole in the first thong. Pull snug. Trim any excess thong.*

For the **running stitch**, continue lacing up and then down through each hole. Pull lacing firm, but not tight, or else the seam will buckle. Most people cinch their lacing tighter than they need to. At the end of the seam you have two choices. You can taper the remaining thong and tie a simple overhand knot, or simply weave the thong back through the underside of the last few stitches. Buckskin has plenty of texture to hold the thong in place.

Other Stitches. The variety of stitches you can do is only limited by your imagination. A great book on lacing is: *Leather Braiding* by Bruce Grant. Cornell Maritime Press, Inc. Centreville, Maryland 21617. We'll show you a few that Michelle and I commonly use. These stitches vary in complexity and take much longer than the running stitch, depending on just how complicated they are:

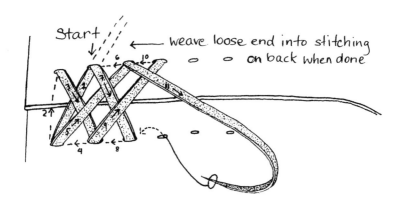

The **herring bone.** This stitch is really beautiful and very time consuming. It's worth it if you like decorative lacing. It can be used to conceal an overlap seam. Your thong should be at least six times as long as the seam. On one piece of buckskin punch two rows of parallel holes. On the other, punch one. The piece with one set of holes is placed on top of the first row on the other. Begin by bringing the lace up through a hole in the *second* row. Then cross over back to a hole in the first row and through. Come back up the other hole in the first row. Then cross over to the empty hole in the second row and through. Your stitching should look like an X. Now the herringbone pattern begins: *"Go directly back one hole. This hole already has a stitch in it. Come up through and cross over to an empty hole. Go directly back one hole, up through it and cross over to an empty hole."* Continue this pattern until complete. Michelle's mantra is *"Up where there is something"*—because the lace comes up through an occupied hole, *"across and down where there is nothing"*—because the lace crosses forward to the next empty hole. The pattern on the underside should look like two straight lines of stitches.

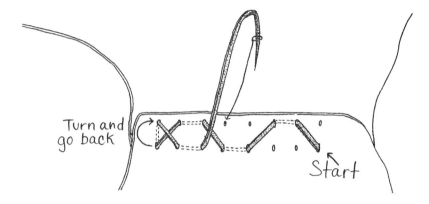

The **X-stitch** is an easy decorative stitch. On one piece of buckskin punch two rows of parallel holes. On the other, punch one. The thong should be about three times the length of the seam. Stitch one thong all the way to the end of the seam, crossing over and skipping a hole with each stitch. Then go back the other way filling in the holes. The underside should look like two rows of the running stitch.

The **saddle stitch.** This stitch is a running stitch that doubles back on itself after reaching the end of the seam. You can use a new thong for the second run. Use the same holes but enter and exit in the opposite direction of the first run. This stitch is particularly for areas that you want to super reinforce and prevent stretch, like buttonholes. It is not necessary in most places as the running stitch is plenty strong.

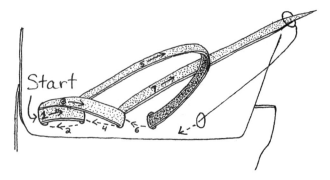

The **french twist**. Poke holes just as you would for the running stitch. The thong should be at least four times the length of the seam. Come out the first hole and go in the second. Come back up the first hole and go in the third. Come back up the second hole and go in the fourth, skip a hole, go in. Continue. *Two holes forward on top and one hole back underneath.* Make sure you always exit the hole from the right of the thong that is already there, or always from the left. The underside will look like a continual line of stitching.

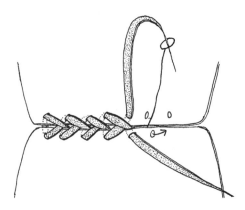

The baseball stitch is used to bring two seams together with no overlap. It is frequently used on shoulder seams where reduced bulk is a plus. Poke a row of holes in each piece of buckskin. Start with either two laces or one folded in half. Bring one end of thong up through each hole in the first row. Then with one thong, cross *under* and up through the next hole on the other side. Then do the same with the other thong. Continue to the other end.

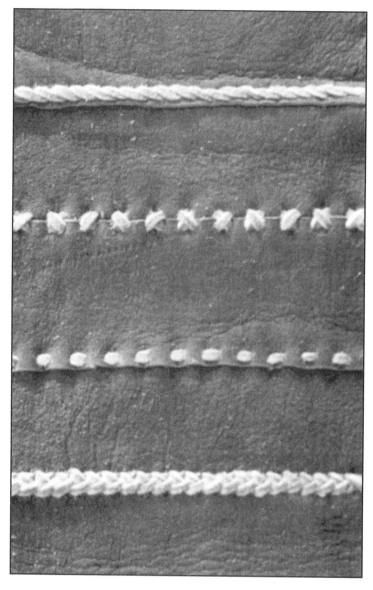

Four lacing stitches for overlapping seams. Top to bottom: **the french twist, the X-stitch, the running stitch** *and* **the herringbone.** *All of these stitches can take on different forms depending on how wide your lacing is and how closely your holes are spaced. These were all done with thin lacing and closely spaced holes. Notice how the herringbone completely covers up the seam.*

Sewing Seams (instead of lacing)

Sewing is faster than lacing because the needle pokes the hole and pulls through at the same time. To sew you need a glover's needle and sinew. The glover's needle and artificial sinew are available at craft shops and Tandy Leather stores. Real sinew is available from along the backbone of a deer (see *Skinning*, p. 43). Regular sewing thread is too weak for hand-stitching, though I

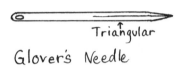

Triangular

Glover's Needle

have seen machine stitched buckskin. You could use thicker and stronger plant fiber cordage, if you can make or find some. (In fact I frequently see garments and moccasins made by Native Americans that are machine stitched. The only folks I've met who do this said they just used a regular machine and needle. It might work great, but try it at your own risk!)

When sewing with a glover's needle it helps to have a thimble or something with which to push the needle through. The smaller the needle that you use the easier it will be to push through, but the more stitches you should make. I usually just wrap a finger with buckskin scraps and push the needle with my finger. You can also use a small piece of wood or buy a specialized needle pusher that is sold at leather craft shops.

Sewing With Sinew

The only time I like to use sinew is on seams that will be hidden on the finished garment because:

(1) Real sinew's weak point is that it wears out through abrasion. With flat seams, abrasion is a constant. With hidden seams the buckskin protects the stitching. Also, when sinew dries out it is rather scratchy against your body.

(2) With a flat seam, artificial sinew will show on the outside of your finished garment. And well,... its just nylon, with a nice name.

Real sinew. Real sinew is more of a diddle to use but worth it because it's the real thing. Sinew is another name for tendons and ligaments. They are composed of the exact same collagen fibers that form buckskin, except that they are arranged linearly rather than irregularly, creating very strong little threads. These fibers attach muscles to bones, giving the muscles control over movement. In many areas of the body a mass of fibers will come together forming a bundle or solid sheet of sinew. The longest sheet of sinew is along the backbone. This sinew has been used to sew human clothing to-gether for millennia.

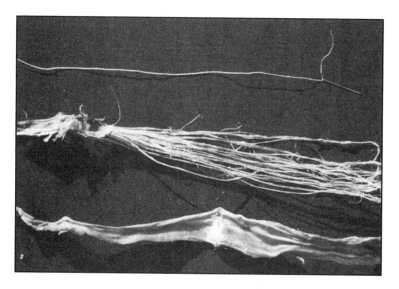

Working sinew from a solid sheet up to the finished thread

Use your fingers to split off a small side of the back-strap sinew. Split this piece in half, then half of that piece in half, until you have it thin enough to thread on your glover's needle, but not much smaller. Thread the thicker end through the needle's eye. You want these threads to be as big as they can be for strength while still being easy to pull through each stitch. Dip your fingers in water and run them along the sinew to moisten, or run the sinew through your moistened lips. Holding one end in your left hand, roll the sinew thread on your right thigh (or vice versa), so that the fibers spiral. You are now ready to sew.

Real sinew is limited in length, and so I prefer not to double over my thread but to use it as a single thickness. Use the same easy knot that is illustrated in the *Sewing* chapter p. 107, for both the start and the finish.

Artificial sinew. Artificial sinew is very easy to use. It is a fast, durable way to sew buckskin. I don't like it because it is artificial and I can't make it myself. You may feel differently.

Artificial sinew comes on spools. It is thicker than it needs to be and it splits down much like real sinew. Cut a length twice as long as you will need. Split this into fourths. Take a fourth, thread it through your glover's needle. Pull it through until the two ends meet and tie them off with an overhand knot. Artificial sinew has a tendency to slip out of knots, so lightly melt the knot with a lit match. When you make your first stitch, come back through the loop formed by

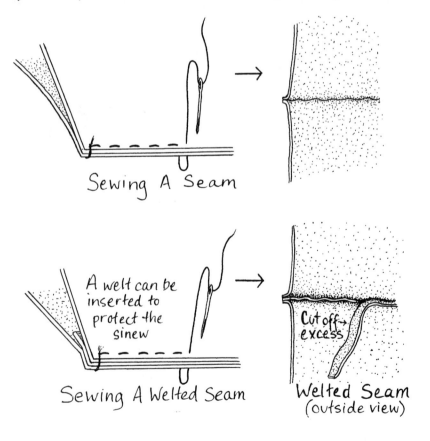

Sewing A Seam

A welt can be inserted to protect the sinew

Sewing A Welted Seam

Cut off→ excess

Welted Seam (outside view)

the knot, and this will lock everything in place.

When you finish your seam. You can either make another overhand knot or the knot that is described in the *Sewing* chapter p. 107 Don't forget to melt it.

Sewing

To start, lay your two pieces together with what will be the outside surfaces, *facing one another*. Make a knot at the beginning of the seam. Use the running stitch and sew to the other end of the seam, taking 1/8 to 1/4 inch stitches about 1/8 to a 1/4 inch from the edge. Knot at the other end. Turn right side out.

Special Effects

Buckskin's resistance to unraveling shows off in these special effects.

The Fringe Element

Buckskin can be cut into long thin strips that hang decoratively from your clothes or pouches. A little thought to function may influence the style of fringe you want. In early Native American cultures long skinny fringe was commonly worn by the horse people of the plains, while shorter tab-like fringe was traditional in the eastern woodlands (presumably to prevent snagging on trees and brush as compared to the windblown freedom and aesthetics the horse riders could enjoy). The plateau cultures typically chose a moderately long tab-style.

Fringe uses up a lot of buckskin, but can be made from scraps. Fringe can either come from extra buckskin that hangs over where you place a seam, or it can be inserted by way of a welt to a flat or a hidden seam. Welted fringe can be made from multiple scraps sewed into the same seam.

There are a couple of particularly poor locations for fringe. Fringe on the lower sleeves can get in the way, dangling in the fire or soup. Fringe on the lower legs collects burrs.

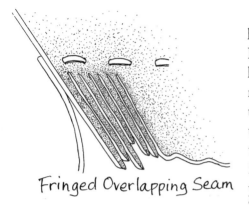

Fringed Overlapping Seam

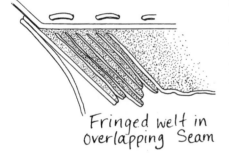

Fringed Welt in Overlapping Seam

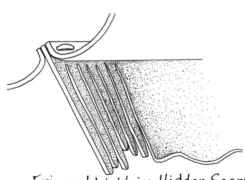

Fringed Welt in Hidden Seam

Cutting fringe. Start at the left side of the future fringe. Hold each new fringe with your left hand, as you cut it with your right. This makes for easier cutting than if you hold your hands the opposite way. Fringe always thins out after you initially cut it. So make it a little wider than you'd like it to be down the trail. This is especially noticeable with thin fringe. Also, fringe cut from thick sections of leather will thin out less than fringe cut from thin leather. If you want it to be of even thickness in the long run, cut the thicker sections narrower than the thinner parts.

Decorating fringe. Anything with a hole in it can be strung on fringe. After you have strung it, put a overhand knot in the fringe to hold the object in place. Some possibilities are shells, pine nuts, dew claws (little deer hooves, that reside above the bigger ones), hollow bones, or any beads.

Why Fringe?

Perhaps humans first decided to fringe their buckskin clothing simply because they could... it was fun... and it's beautiful. Here are some other explanations I've run across.

'fringe is a sign of wealth'. Who but the rich native could take such a useful commodity, cut it into shreds and hang it from their clothing? Perhaps one of the earliest cases of conspicuous consumption.

'fringe wicks water away from your body, keeping you drier'. If buckskin gets wet, it gets soaked. You aren't going to wear soaked buckskins long enough to have this make a meaningful difference. Pure poppycock in my opinion.

'fringe breaks up your human form, creating camouflage'. The deer, moose, elk and buffalo family can see form and movement but not detail. By having fringe moving around on your form, you could blend in more like the grasses or leaves on a tree. On the other hand the movement of fringe might alert the deer to your presence on still days...

'fringe provides useful emergency cordage'.

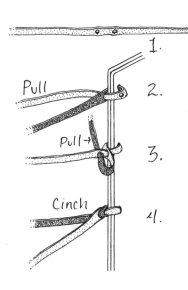

Tassels

Tassels are long thongs that can hang from anywhere on your buckskin. They can also function as stitching if placed close together on seams. To cinch them in place, make two holes in the buckskin, where you want the tassels to hang. Put two holes near the center of the future tassel. Lace through the holes on your garment until the two tassel holes are on different sides. Lace

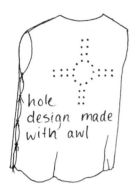

hole
design made
with awl

each loose end through the hole in the other loose end and cinch.

Decorative Holes

I recently saw an old picture of an Indian man who had poked large awl holes in a pattern across the front of his buckskin shirt. Not only did this look interesting but it would create more ventilation for hot weather clothes. Turns out that this is a very common element on Plains Indian shirts. You could only get away with this with buckskin.

Pigment and Dyes

Many native peoples rubbed colored clays and powders into their buckskin, giving them a large selection of colors. Some garments would be one color on the yoke, another on the sleeves, and yet another on the fringe. The pigment would have to be renewed periodically. Pigmented clays and powders were actually used as a means of 'washing' clothes as they would absorb oils and associated debris which could then be shaken out. You can also dye your buckskin with tannin dyes to give it a brown, black, yellow, or reddish hue. See Edholm and Wilder's *"Wet-scrape Braintanned Buckskin"* for more on dyeing buckskin.

Washing Buckskin

Treat buckskin as you would your own skin. Don't get it too hot. It is not stable over 120 degrees. It will turn into smoked bucca skinneolies, a famous and delicious pasta dish. While this dish is truly fantastic, and loved by starving people the world over, it may not be what you want to do with your first hides. If the water is too hot for your skin, it is too hot for your buckskin.

Washing

Use cold or warm water and mild soaps. It is probably best to wash by hand and use a scrub brush. Buckskin can stand up to vigorous scrubbing and wringing. I must come clean and confess that I have often washed my skin clothes in a machine with ghastly detergents like Tide, and have had no problems whatsoever, aside from my fringe being tied into knots. It is better to use mild soaps though, because they replace some of the oils that they strip. This is important because buckskin likes to have some oils in it as does your skin or any leather.

Accidentally boiled your buckskins?

After many washings you can soak your skins in a mix of Ivory Soap and pure neat's foot oil, (available at farm and feed stores). An eighth of a cup of oil to a gallon of water is a good ratio. This creates an oil emulsion that will replenish the oils in your buckskin without getting them oily. I've tried re-soaking them in brains but that did not seem to do as good of a job. Don't oil them as you would leather. This just makes buckskin oily.

Drying

Do not dry in a machine drier! It will permanently shrink your clothing. Instead, lay your garments out flat, or hang them from a line. When they are dry, they will feel like line dried linen or overly starched underwear. Simply stretch them in all directions, and they will become soft. This should not take but a minute or two. This is the minimum you need to do.

To return your skin garments completely to that luscious feel, it helps to abrade the surfaces. Similarly to linen or hemp, the little outer fibers stiffen up in the course of drying and won't soften just from the hand stretching. I usually cable the inside surface of my clothes, because the cable abrasion pattern won't show there and its fast. Then I lightly pumice the outer surface. This really makes them feel good, and that's what its all about. This is the primo treatment, however, and a simple one-two pull over the corner of a chair will also do the job.

Another technique is to lightly stretch your clothes while they are still a bit damp. This will help them dry soft. The best thing to do is to don your shirt or pants and wear them until dry. This will give them the ultimate custom fit, though not an advisable practice in freezing weather.

Bibliography

This bibliography has a few extra features to help you in your research. Titles have been arranged into subject areas for easy reference. Comments on books that are of particular interest are denoted by the ☞ symbol. These comments include: the dates historic references were actually gathered, particularly interesting information available in the work, or simply the fact that the resource doesn't have much information in it and might not be worth your time pursuing.

Tanning Guides

Churchill, James. *The Complete Guide to Tanning Skins and Furs.* Mechanicsburg, PA: Stackpole Books, 1983.
  ☞ Good breadth, poor depth. Covers a lot of methods and skin types.
Edholm, Steven and Wilder, Tamara. *Buckskin: The Ancient Art of Brain Tanning.* Boonville, CA: Paleotechnics, 1997
  ☞ Excellent work that is worth getting if you have a strong interest in brain tanning.
Farnham, A.B. *Home Tanning and Leather Making Guide.* Columbus OH: A.R. Harding Publishing Co, 1950.
Goodchild, Peter. *Survival Skills of the North American Indians.* Chicago: Chicago Review Press, 1984.
Hobson, Phyllis. *Tan Your Hide!* Pownal VT: Garden Way Publishing, 1977.
  ☞ Nowhere near enough detail to have much chance of success
McPherson, John. *Brain Tan Buckskin.* Lawrence, KS: Prairie Wolf, 1986.
Riggs, Jim. *Blue Mountain Buckskin: A Working Manual.* Wallowa, OR: 1979.
  ☞ Best guide to the 'dry scrape' method.
Schaefer, Arlington C. *The Indian Art of Tanning Buckskin.* Roseburg OR: Schaefer-Knudtson Publications, 1973.

Leather Chemistry

Beinkiewicz, Krzysztof J. *Physical Chemistry of Leather Making.* Malabar FL: Kreiger publishing Co, 1983.

Cormack, David. *An Introduction to Histology.* 1984.
☛ Gives you an understanding of skin structure and elements from an anatomical point of view. Really helped me understand more of what the chemistry books were talking about.

Davis, Charles Thomas. *The Manufacture of Leather.* Philadelphia: Henry Carey Baird & Co.

Dutta, S.S. *An Introduction to the Principles of Leather Manufacture.* Lalbazar India: The Indian Leather Technologists Association.

Haines, Betty. *The Microstructure of Collagen.*

Lazell, E.W. *Hydrated Lime: History, Manufacture and Uses in Plaster, Mortar, and Concrete.* Pittsburgh PA: Jackson-Remlinger Publishing Co, 1915.

O'Flaherty, Fred. *Chemistry and Technology of Leather.* New York: Reinhold Publishing Corp, 1956.
☛ A collection of articles. Fairly technical but very good.

Progress in Leather Science 1920-1945. London:British Leather Manufacturers Association, 1948.

Reed, R. *Ancient Skins, Parchment and Leather.* London: Seminar Press, 1972.
☛ Highly recommended, must read for anyone interested in ancient tanning processes. Good in depth discussion of the chemistry of traditional tanning methods, that is fully understandable to the lay man. This book increased my understanding of brain tanning many fold.

Thorstensen, Thomas C. *Practical Leather Technology.* New York: Van Nostrand Reinhold Co, 1969.

Wilson, John Arthur. *The Chemistry of Leather Manufacture.* New York: The Chemical Catalog Co, 1923.

Pioneer America

Austin, Maria. Letter to Her Son Stephen, in Texas. Jan. 16, 1822. Braund, Kathryn E. Holland. *Deerskins and Duffels.* Lincoln & London: University of Nebraska Press, 1993.

Cunningham, Patricia A. & Lab, Susan Vose. *Dress in American Culture.* Bowling Green: Bowling Green State University Popular Press, 1993.

Evans, Mary. *How to Make Historic American Costumes.* New York: A.S. Barnes & Co., 1942.

Holley, Mary Austin. *Texas.* 1836.

Holman, David & Persons, Billie. *Buckskin and Homespun: Frontier Texas Clothing, 1820-1870,* Austin: Wind River Press, 1979.

Pitz, Henry C. & Warwick, Edward & Wyckoff, Alexander. *Early American Dress: The Colonial and Revolutionary Period.* New York: Benjamin Blom Publishers, 1965.

Postlethewayt, Malachye. *"The Universal Dictionary of Trade and Commerce".* 1774.

Taylor, Walter Penn. *The Deer of North America.* Harrisburg PA: The Stackpole Co, 1956.

Wilcox, R. Turner. *Five Centuries of American Costume.* New York: Charles Scribner's Sons, 1963.

Native Americans

Northwest Coast

Barnett, Homer G. *The Coast Salish of British Columbia*. Eugene: University of Oregon Press, 1955.

Boas, Franz. *"The Kwakiutl of Vancouver Island"*. Memoirs of the American Museum of Natural History Vol VIII, Part II. New York: G.E. Stechert, 1909.

Drucker, Philip. *"Northwest Coast"*. Anthropology Records, Culture Element Distributions: XXVI. Berkeley: University of California Press,1950.

Elmendorf, William J. & Kroeber, A.L.. *Twana Culture*. Washington: Washington State University Press, 1960.

Emmons, George Thornton. *The Tlingit Indians*. Seattle & London: University of Washington Press, 1991.

Gunther, Erna. *"Klallam Ethnography"*. University of Washington Publications in Anthropology Vol 1, #5. Seattle: University of Washington Press, 1927.

Teit, James. *"The Thompson Indians of British Columbia"*. Memoirs of the American Museum of Natural History Vol II, pt. IV. New York: G.E. Stechert, 1900.
☛ Original manuscript written 1895.

Teit, James. *"The Lilloet Indians"*. Memoirs of the American Museum of Natural History Vol IV, pt. V. New York: G.E. Stechert, 1906.

Teit, James. *"The Shuswap"*. Memoirs of the American Museum of Natural History Vol II, pt. VII. New York: G.E. Stechert, 1900.
☛ Based on interviews with elders from 1888 to 1900.

Plateau

Albright, Sylvia L. *"Tahltan Ethnoarchaeology"*. Department of Archeology Publication #15. Burnaby BC: Simon Fraser University, 1984.

Emmons, G.T. *"The Tahltan Indians"*. Anthropological Publications of the University of Pennsylvania Museum, Vol III. Philadelphia: The University Museum, 1911.
☛ Interesting details on neolithic tools.

Holbert, Harry. *"Ethnography of the Kootenai"*. Memoirs of the American Anthropological Association #56. Menasha, WI: American Anthropological Association, 1941.

Peltier, Jerome. *Manners and Customs of the Coeur D'Alene Indians*. Spokane: Peltier Publishing.

Post, Richard & Commonst, Rachel S. *"The Sinkaietk or Southern Okanogan"*. General Series in Anthropology #6. Menasha, WI: George Banta Publishing Co., 1938.

Ray, Verne F. *"Plateau"*, Anthropological Records Vol 8 #2, Culture Element Distributions XXII. Berkeley: University of California Press, 1942.

Sapir, Edward & Spier, Leslie. *"Wishram Ethnography"*, University of Washington Publications in Anthropology Vol 3, #3. Seattle: University of Washington Press, 1930.

Spinden, Herbert Joseph. *"The Nez Perce Indians"*. Memoirs of the American Anthropological Association Vol II, Part III. Lancaster PA: New Era Printing Company, 1908.

Teit, James. *"The Salishan Tribes of the Western Plateaus"*, Bureau of American Ethnology 45th Annual Report. Washington: US Government Printing Office, 1930.

Plains

Catlin, George. *North American Indians: Being letters and notes on their manners, customs, and conditions, written during eight years' travel amongst the wildest tribes of Indians in North America, 1832-1839.* Philadelphia: Leary, Stuart and Co., 1913.
☞ One of the earliest (1830's) detailed accounts of Plains Indian tanning. Specifies the use of a wood-ash lye as part of the '*usual mode of dressing the buffalo, and other skins...*'

Denig. *"The Assiniboine".* Bureau of American Ethnology Annual Report #46. Washington: US Government Printing Office, 1928.

Desmet. *"Assiniboine of the Forest",* Anthropological Papers of the American Museum of Natural History Vol IV. New York: G.E. Stechert, 1909.

Dodge, Colonel Richard Irving. *Our Wild Indians: Thirty-three Years Personal Experience Among the Red Men of the Great West.* Hartford: A.D. Worthington and Co., 1883.
☞ Based on experiences from the 1840's to 1870's. Third earliest detailed account of Plains tanning, specifies the use of a wood-ash lye soak as a basic step in tanning buffalo skins and making parfleche.

Dorsey, J. Owen. *"Omaha Sociology".* Bureau of American Ethnology Annual Report #3. Washington: US Government Printing Office, 1881.

Ewers, John C. *The Blackfeet: Raiders on the Western Plains.* Norman OK: University of Oklahoma Press, 1958.

Fletcher, A.C. & LaFlesche, F. *"The Omaha Tribe",* Bureau of American Ethnology Annual Report #27. Washington: US Government Printing Office, 1905.

Grinnel, George Bird. *The Cheyenne Indians: Their History and Ways of Life.* New York: Cooper Square Publishers, 1962.
☞ Based on experiences 1890-1923.

Hanson, James Austin. *Metal Weapons, Tools and Ornaments of the Teton Dakota Indians.* Lincoln NE: University of Nebraska Press, 1975.

Hoebbel, E. Adamson. *The Cheyennes: Indians of the Great Plains.* New York: Harcourt, Brace, Johanovich College Publishers, 1960.

Hoebbel, E. Adamson & Wallace, Ernest. *The Comanches.* Norman OK: University of Oklahoma Press, 1955.

Howard, James H. *"The Ponca Tribe".* Bulletin of the Bureau of American Ethnology #195. Washington: US Government Printing Office, 1965,

Hunter, John D. *Memoirs of Captivity Among the Indians of North American (from Childhood to the Age of Nineteen).* London: 1823.
☞ Based on experiences at the end of the 1700's and beginning of the 1800's. This is the earliest detailed account of Plains hide tanning I've found. Specifies the use of a wood-ash lye soak as part of the basic tanning methods, plus has all kinds of interesting tanning details and materials—especially for Buffalo. Great read.

Kroeber, Alfred L. *"The Arapaho".* Bulletin of the American Museum of Natural History Vol XVIII. Lincoln & London: University of Nebraska Press, 1902.

Lowie, Robert H. *"The Assiniboine".* Anthropological Papers of the American Museum of Natural History Vol IV. New York: G.E. Stechert, 1909.

Lowie, Robert H. *The Crow Indians.* New York: Farrar & Rinehart Inc., 1935.

Lowie, Robert H. *Indians of the Plains.* Garden City NY: The Natural History Press, 1954.

Mandelbaum, David G. *"The Plains Cree"*. Canadian Plains Series. Regina: University of Regina Occasional Publications, 1979.

Mails, Thomas E. *The Mystic Warriors of the Plains*. Garden City, NY: Doubleday & Co. Inc., 1972.

Powers, William K. *Indians of the Northern Plains*. 1969. Skinner, Alanson. *"Ethnology of the Ioway Indians"*. Bulletin of the Public Museum of Milwaukee Vol 5, #4. Milwaukee: The Public Museum of Milwaukee, 1926.

Skinner, Alanson. *"The Eastern Cree"*, Anthropological Papers of the American Museum of Natural History Vol IX. New York: G.E. Stechert, 1911.

Steward, Dr. Julian. *The Blackfoot*. Berkeley: US Department of the Interior, National Park Service Field Division of Education, 1934.

Weltfish, Gene. *The Lost Universe*. New York: Ballantine Books, 1965.
   ☞ Based on interviews with elders in the 1920's

Wissler, Clark. *"Material Culture of the Blackfoot Indians"*, Anthropological Papers of the American Museum of Natural History Vol V, Part I. New York: G.E. Stechert, 1910.

Wissler, Clark. *North American Indians of the Plains*. New York: American Museum of Natural History, 1920.

Great Basin

Fowler, Don C. *"Material Culture of the Numa"*, Smithsonian Contributions to Anthropology #26. Washington: Smithsonian Institute Press, 1979.

Kelly, Isabel T. *"Ethnography of the Surprise Valley Paiute"*, University of California Publications in American Archaeology and Ethnology Vol 31. Berkeley: University of California Press, 1932.

Lowie, Robert H. *"Shoshonean Ethnography"*, Anthropological Papers of the American Museum of Natural History Vol XX. New York: G.E. Stechert, 1924.

Lowie, Robert H. *"The Northern Shoshone"*, Anthropological Papers of the American Museum of Natural History Vol II. New York: AMS Press Inc, 1909.

Ray, Verne F. *Primitive Pragmatists: The Modoc Indians of Northern California*. Seattle: University of Washington Press, 1963.

Riddell. *Honey Lake Paiute Ethnography*. Steward, Julian H. *"Nevada Shoshoni"*, Anthropological Records Vol 4, #2: Cultural Element Distributions XIII. Berkeley: University of California Press, 1941.

Steward, Julian H. *" Northern & Gosiute Shoshone"*, Anthropological Records Vol 8, #3: Cultural Element Distribution XXIII. Berkeley: University of California Press, 1943.

Stewart, Omar C. *"Northern Paiute"*, Anthropological Records Vol 4, #3: Cultural Element Distributions XIV. Berkeley: University of California Press, 1936.

Stewart, Omar C. *"Ute - Southern Paiute"*, Anthropological Records Vol 6, #4: Cultural Element Distributions XVIII. Berkeley: University of California Press, 1942.

Southwest

Buskirk, Winfred. *The Western Apache: Living With the Land before 1950*. Norman OK & London: University of Oklahoma Press, 1986.

Ferg, Alan & Kessel, William. *Western Apache Material Culture: The Goodwin and Guenther Collections*. Tucson: University of Arizona Press, 1987.

Geronimo (edited by Barrett, S.M.). *Geronimo: His Own Story.* New York: E.P. Dutton & Co., 1970.

☛ Based on what Geronimo dictated to Asa Daklugie in 1904-05. Geronimo states that 'During my minority (youth) we had never seen a missionary or a priest. We had never seen a white man'. A very interesting autobiographical account with a good helping of material culture. His description of deerskin tanning starts with soaking the hides in a wood-ash lye.

Gifford, E.W. *"Apache-Pueblo",* Anthropological Records Vol 4, #1: Culture Element Distributions XII. Berkeley: University of California Press, 1940.

Gifford, E.W. *"Northeastern and Western Yavapai",* University of California Publications in American Archaeology and Ethnology Vol 34, #4. Berkeley: University of California Press, 1936.

Gifford, E.W. *"The Southeastern Yavapai",* University of California Publications in American Archaeology and Ethnography. Berkeley: University of California Press.

Haley, James L. *Apaches: A History and Culture Portrait.* Garden City NY: Doubleday & Co, 1981.

Hill, W.W. *An Ethnography of the Santa Clara Pueblo, New Mexico.* Albuquerque: University of New Mexico Press, 1982.

Lange, Charles H. *Cochiti: A New Mexico Pueblo Past and Present.* Austin: University of Texas Press, 1959.

Mails, Thomas E. *The People Called Apache.* New York: BDD Illustrated Books, 1971.

Mason, Otis. *Report of the National Museum: Aboriginal Skin-Dressing.* Washington: National Museum, 1889.

Opler, Morris Edward. *An Apache Lifeway: The Economic, Social and ReligiousInstitutions of the Chiricahua Indians.* New York: Cooper Square Publishers, 1965.

Roberts, Frank H.H. *"Village of the Great Kivas on the Zuni Reservation, New Mexico",* Bureau of American Ethnology Vol 111. Washington: US Government Printing Office, 1932.

Russell, Frank. *The Pima Indians.* With introd., citation sources, and bibliography by Bernard L. Fontana. Tucson, Ariz.: University of Arizona Press, 1975. - XV, 479 pp. : Ill.

Spier, Leslie. *"Havasupai Ethnography",* Anthropological Papers of the American Museum of Natural History Vol XXIX part III. New York: G.E. Stechert, 1928.

Underhill, Ruth. *Pueblo Crafts.* Washington: Bureau of Indian Affairs, 1944.

Eastern Woodlands

Brereton, John. *Sailors Narratives Along the New England Coast, With Notes by George Parker Winship.* New York, Burt Franklin, 1905.

☛ Originally written in 1602, very little detail.

Densmore, Francis. *"Chippewa Customs",* Bureau of American Ethnology Bulletin 86. Washington: US Government Printing Office, 1929.

Hilger, Sister M. Ines. *"Chippewa Child Life",* Bureau of American Ethnology Bulletin 146. Washington: US Government Printing Office, 1951.

King, William S. *Iroquois Crafts.* Lawrence KS: Publications Service of the Haskell Institute,

Lyford, Carrie A. *"Ojibwa Crafts",* Bureau of Indian Affairs, Indian Handcraft Series. 1943.

Morgan, Lewis H. *League of the Iroquois*. New York: Mead & Co, 1922.
☛ Originally written in 1851. Not a lot of detail, but some.

Morton, Thomas. *"Manners and Customs of the Indians, An Extract for his New English Canaan"*. Old South Leaflets Vol IV. Boston: Directors of the Old South Meeting House.
☛ Originally written in 1637...not much detail.

Ritzenthaler, Robert. *"The Chippewa Indian Method of Securing and Tanning Deerskin"*. Wisconsin Archaeologist Vol 28, #1.
☛ Good detail and pictures of Chippewa women in different stages of tanning.

Skinner, Alanson. *"The Northern Saulteaux"*. Anthropological Papers of the American Museum of Natural History Vol IX. New York: 1911.

Skinner, Alanson. *"Prairie Potawatomi Indians Part II, Notes on the Material Culture"*. Bulletin of the Public Museum of Milwaukee Vol VI. Milwaukee: 1926.

Skinner, Alanson. *"Ethnology of the Sauk Indians"*. Bulletin of the Public Museum of Milwaukee Vol V. Milwaukee: 1925.

Skinner, Alanson. *"Material Culture of the Menomini"*. Indian Notes & Monographs. New York: Museum of the American Indian, Heye Foundation, 1921.
☛ Good detailed account, with many pictures of Menomini women in different stages of tanning.

Southeast

Bushnell, James H. *"The Choctaw of Bayou Lacomb, Louisiana"*. Bureau of American Ethnology, Bulletin 48. Washington: Government Printing Office, 1909.

Lawson, John. *A New Voyage to Carolina*. Chapel Hill: University of North Carolia Press, 1967.
☛ Originally written in 1860. Talks about the common use of sweet corn as a substitute for brains, and the Native use of tannins.

Swanton, John R. *"Indians of the Southeastern United States"*. Bureau of American Ethnology, Bulletin 137. Washington: Government Printing Office, 1946.
☛ Great source on tanning in the southeast, with many primary source references from the 1700's and 1800's.

California

Aginsky, B.W. *"Central Sierra"*. Anthropological Records Vol 8, #4: Cultural Element Distributions XXIV. Berkeley: University of California Press, 1943.

Ayer, Gladys. *" Bear River Ethnography"*. Anthropological Records Vol 2, #2. Berkeley: University of California Press, 1938.

Barrett, S.A. & Gifford, E.W. *" Miwok Material Culture: Indian Life of the Yosemite Region"*. Bulletin of Milwaukee Public Museum Vol 2, #4. Milwaukee: 1933.

Drucker, Philip. *"Yuman-Piman"*. Anthropological Records Vol 6, #3: Culture Element Distributions XVII.Berkeley: University of California Press, 1941.

Essene, Frank. *"Round Valley"*. Anthropological Records Vol 8, #1: Culture Element Distributions XXI. Berkeley: University of California Press, 1942.

Garth, Thomas R. *"Atsugewi Ethnography"*. Anthropological Records Vol 14, #2. Berkeley: University of California Press, 1953.

Gayton, A.H. *"Yokuts and Western Mono Ethnography"*. Anthropological Records Vol 10, #1. Berkeley: University of California Press, 1948.

Gifford, E.W. & Klimek, Stanislaw. *"Culture Element Distributions II: Yana"*. University of California Publications in American Archaeology and Ethnology Vol 37, #2. Berkeley: University of California Press, 1936.

Holt, Catharine. *"Shasta Ethnography"*. Anthropological Records Vol 3, #4. Berkeley: University of California Press, 1946.

Voegelin, Erminie W. *"NE California"*. Anthropological Records Vol 7, #2: Culture Element Distributions XX. Berkeley: University of California Press, 1940.

Voegelin, Erminie W. *"Tübatulabal Ethnography"*. Anthopological Records Vol 2, #1. Berkeley: University of California Press, 1938.

Arctic and Subarctic

Honismann, *"Culture and Ethos of Kaska Society"*. Yale University Publications in Anthropology, 40.

Murdoch, John. *"Ethnological Results of the Point Barrow Expedition"*. Bureau of Ethnology Annual Report #9. 1887.

☞ Quite long, detailed and fascinating. The Inuit tools and methods are fairly unique. Well described and illustrated.

Nelson, Edward William. *"The Eskimo About Bering Straight"*. Bureau of American Ethnology 18th Annual Report. Washington: US Government Printing Office, 1896.

Oakes, Jillian E. *"Copper and Caribou Inuit Skin Clothing Production"*. Canadian Ethnology Service Mercury Series Paper # 118. Hull, Quebec: Canadian Museum of Civilization, 1991.

☞ Written in 1944. Relatively long, detailed and interesting step by step discussion of the tanning of Caribou skins for clothing.

Powell, J.W. *"The Hudson Bay Eskimo"*. Bureau of Ethnology 11th Annual Report. Washington: US Government Printing Office, 1889.

☞ Shows interesting tools for applying paints to skins.

Rogers, Edward S. *"The Material Culture of the Mistassini"*. National Museum of Canada Bulletin #218, Anthro Series #80. Ottawa: 1967.

Miscellaneous Accounts

Binford, *"Smudge Pits"* American Antiquity Vol 32, #1. 1967.

☞ Detailed analysis of smoking pits used east of the Mississippi.

Bogoras, W. *"The Chukchee Material Culture"*. Memoirs of the American Museum of Natural History Vol XI Part 1. New York: G.E. &Stechert Co, 1909.

☞ Very interesting account of native tanning methods in Siberian Russia. Doesn't mention brains but similar elements are used, and some dis-similar. Fairly long, fairly detailed, good drawings of tools.

Driver, Harold E. *Indians of North America*. Chicago: University of Chicago Press, 1961.

Faber, G.A. *"Greek and Roman Tanners"*. The Ciba Review, May 1938. Basle.

Handbook of the North American Indians Vol 10: Southwest. Washington: Smithsonian Institute, 1983.

Hodge, Frederick Webb. *Handbook of the American Indians, North of Mexico, Part 2*. Washington: Government Printing Office, 1910.

King, Arden Ross. *Aboriginal Skin Dressing in Western North America.* Unpublished PHD Dissertation: University of California at Berkeley, 1947.

☛ A book length cataloguing and analysis of the archaeological and anthropological record. Great source for finding a lot of the data in one place, a lot of his analysis is quite interesting though much of it is faulty in my opinion. I don't think he ever tanned a hide, or really understood the process. Only available at UC Berkeley.

Mason, Otis. *Report of the National Museum: Aboriginal Skin Dressing.* 1889.

☛ An oft quoted resource, that is reasonably interesting.

Paterek, Joseph. *The Encyclopedia of American Indian Costume.* Santa Barbara: ABC-CLIO Publishing, 1994.

Shwerz, F. *"Leather Dressing in the Stone Age".* The Ciba Review, April 1938. Basle.

☛ Some interesting detail about stone age tanning throughout the world, some of it to be taken with a grain of salt.

Steinburg, Jack. *The Manufacture and Use of Bone Defleshing Tools.* American Antiquity Vol 31, #4. 1966.

Vaughan-Kirby, F. *"Zululand: Skin-dressing".* Man: A Monthly Record of Anthropological Science Vol 18. Royal Anthropological Institute of Great Britain and Ireland, 1918.

Wilder, Edna. *Secrets of Eskimo Skin Sewing.* Anchorage AK: Alaska Northwest Publishing Co, 1976.

☛ Talks about the use of alder bark tannins in traditional Eskimo fur tanning, includes some traditional patterns, and fur sewing techniques.

Young, Stella. *Navajo Native Dyes: Their Preparation and Use by Nonabah G. Bryan, Navajo.* US Department of the Interior: Bureau of Indian Affairs, 1940.

About the Author

M att Richards lives with his wife Michelle and daughters Hazel & Eliza on a ranch at the base of the Siskyou Mountains of SW Oregon. They tan and teach hide tanning for a living (and clothing); and enjoy hunting, gathering wild edibles, gardening and going for a swim in the river.

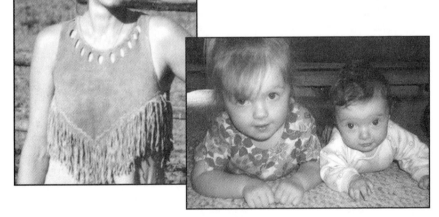

Resource Directory

This resource directory is designed to help you find local hands-on instruction, tools, books and videos, custom garment designers or more tanned buckskin (you can never have too much). Some of these folks have been tanning for twenty to thirty years. They are teachers, peers, friends or simply talented people with something to offer. Every class, tool and product in here is made of natural buckskin, most of it brain tan. Keep in mind that most of these folks are home producers rather than industrial conglomerates and may not always have what you want in stock. It may take a call or two, but you should be able to find what you are looking for. You will notice that each person is listed as either wet scrape, dry scrape, or both. Wet scrape is the method taught in this book. Dry scrape is done by drying the hide out on a frame and shearing off the hair and grain with a sharp tool. The process and product are slightly different but not much.

Classes

There is probably someone near you who teaches tanning classes. I highly recommend getting some hands-on instruction. Tanning is such a tactile art that there is a lot someone experienced can show you in person that a book just can't. Some instructors will teach a slightly different method.

Tools

Scrapers, cables, pumice and KOH are available through the *Traditional Tanner's Supply.*

Books and Videos

Several other books and a few videos have been written on brain tanning. From them you can gain more tips, ideas and other approaches to the buckskin craft.

Finished Skins

If you want more buckskin than you have the time or resources to tan yourself, then you can get some from many of the folks listed.

Custom Garments

There are talented folks out there who can turn your or their finished skins into beautiful clothing, pouches, quivers and more.

Other

Buffalo robes, hide tipis, internships...

Matt and Michelle Richards
1700 East Nevada St
Ashland OR 97520
www.braintan.com
matt@braintan.com
wet scrape: sells **finished skins**, teaches **classes with** modern or all traditional/**primitive tools**, makes **custom garments**.

Tom and Nancy Oar
38700 Yaak River Rd.
Troy, MT. 59935
406-295-5167
both methods: sell **finished skins** of deer, antelope, bighorn sheep and **brain tanned furs** of mtn. lion, otter, buffalo and more. makes **custom garments.**

River Spirit School of Natural Living
P.O. Box 173
Mad River, CA. 95552
both methods: teaches **classes**, makes **custom garments**, sells finished skins.

Don Born
9544 Waterbury Dr.
Peyton, CO. 80831
(719) 495-8826
Email dborn@d20.co.edu
wet scrape: sells **finished hides** of deer and elk.

Dave and Marla Bethke
3149 W. Rast Road
American Falls, ID 83211
208-226-2709
wet scrape: teaches classes, sells **finished skins**, **pouches** and garments.

Doug Crist
1501 Dodge Creek
Rexford, MT 59930
wet scrape: sells finished **skins**, teaches
classes, makes **custom garments.**

Teaching Drum Outdoor School
7124 Military Road
Three Lakes, WI 54562
715-546-2944
E-Mail: tdrums-2@new north.net
www.newnorth.net/tdrums2
wet scrape: teaches **classes**, sells **finished
skins**. various books and videos on
either method.

Mike & Sue Rider
Dirty Shirt Buckskins
2263 Gold Creek Ridge Rd
Sandpoint ID 83864
208-265-4862
wet scrape: sells **finished skins, custom
garments, porcupine quill work,** and
teaches classes.

Brian Jensen
26412 Oak Meadow Dr.
WestPerrysburg, OH 43551
419-874-4600
dry scrape: teaches **classes,** makes
custom garments. Specializes in Native
American style plains **beadwork,** 30 yrs
experience.

Hofunee Programs —Scott Jones
The Woods
Rt. 1, Box 182-A
Carlton, GA 30627
706-743-5144
dry scrape: teaches **classes,** sells finished
skins when available. Also offers
internships.

Charlie Trujillo
P.O. Box 499
Clark Fork, ID 83811
208-266-1308
wet scrape: sells finished **skins** and
Native American crafts

Brent Sasquatch Ladd
11642 E. 1050 N.
Otterbein, In 47970
765-583-2301
wet scrape: teaches **classes,** sells **finished
skins** and makes **custom garments.**

Billy Metcalf
1930 Snowball Ck. E.,
Grand Forks BC, V0H 1H1, Canada
Phone (250) 442-5642
Email: billymetcalf@hotmail.com
wet scrape: Sells **finished deerskins,**
smoked or white.

Hollowtop Outdoor Primitive School
Box 691
Pony, MT 59747-0691
406-685-3222
tomelpel@3rivers.net
wet scrape: teaches **classes.**

Michael Foltmer
1330 Brantner Rd.
Greeley, CO 80634
970-339-5608
wet scrape: teaches **classes,** makes
custom garments and sells **finished
skins.** Sometimes dry scrapes.

Duztin Sorensen
P.O. Box 84
Henrieville, UT 84736
435-679-8415
wet scrape: sells **finished hides.**

Frank and Karen Sherwood
Earthwalk Northwest
P.O. Box 461
Issaquah, WA 98027
206-746-7267
Fax 206-746-7757
both methods: teach **classes.**

Ways of our Ancestors
Richie Taylor
4674 Chestatee Heights Rd,
Gainesville GA 30506
770-889-7959
RGTAYLOR58@aol.com
hometown.aol.com/rgtaylor58/
myhomepage/business.html
both methods: teaches **classes** sells
finished hides. Makes **custom garments** and accessories.

Sundog Traders
Joseph Dinsmore & Victoria Longtrail
D.POB 182
Winnett, Montana 59087
Phone: 406-429-7828
Email: ezra@midrivers.com
wet scrape: pre-smoking method.
Classes year round at $75 per day,
finished skins, and **custom garments.**

Paleotechnics
Steven Edholm and Tamara Wilder
P.O. Box 876
Boonville, CA 95415
707-793-2287 (voice-mail)
www.paleotechnics.com
wet scrape: authors of the book
*"Buckskin: The Ancient Art of Brain
Tanning".* They teach **classes** on brain
tanning, fur tanning, and advanced
brain tanning.

Wes Housler
22 Bell Canyon
Cloudcroft, N.M. 88317
505-687-3267
both methods: makes **custom garments**
including buffalo hide moccasins with
the hair inside (I got a pair!), sells
finished wet scraped **skins** of deer and
elk. Also dry scrapes **buffalo robes,**
and **rawhide.**

Sioux Replications
Mr. & Mrs. Larry Belitz
HCR 52, Box 176
Hot Springs, SD 57747-9609
605-745-3902
dry scrape: makes **custom garments,**
sells **finished skins** and the **book**
"Braintanning the Sioux Way". Also
tans elk and buffalo skins; **museum
replications** and **buffalo hide tipis.**

Randy & Lori Breeuwsma
12137-85 Street
Edmonton, Alberta, Canada T5B 3G5
403-474-5405
Email: randy@karamat.com
Website: www.karamat.com
both methods: **Buffalo, Moose, Elk
and Deer. Hair on or off,** smoked or
white. **Hide tipi's to moccasins.**

Bob Kursawe
Bows & Buckskins
860 496-8623
bobkarchery@snet.net
www.buckskintanner.com
wet scrape: sells **brain tanned hides,**
bags, purses & pouches (some
clothing). Will Custom tan your hides.
Teaches **classes** in Connecticut.

Jim Miller
962 F30
Mikado, MI 48745
wet and dry scrape: teaches **classes** (deer, furs, buffalo) sells **finished skins**, **booklet** *"Brain Tan Buffalo Robes, Skins And Pelts"*.

Prairie Wolf
John and Geri McPherson
Box 96 Randolph, KS 66554
dry scrape: **book** "Braintan Buckskin" $3 plus shipping .

Woods Wisdom
P.O. Box 228
Fayetteville, Pa 17222-0228
717-352-8499
dry scrape: teaches **classes.**

Cody Lundin
Aboriginal Living Skills School
P.O. Box 3064
Prescott, AZ 86302
520-776-1342
wet scrape: teaches two days **classes**, hides and tools provided.

Ken Woody
Box 602
Beulah, N.D. 58523
701-873-4999
Email Klwood@westriv.com
both methods: teaches **classes**, sells scraping **tools**, makes **custom garments**, sells **finished skins**. Also does buffalo, N. Plains museum replicas, **buffalo hide tipis**.

Classes with Matt Richards

Join us on our ranch in southern Oregon for a weekend of hide tanning. Matt guides you step by step as you take a skin all the way through the tanning process and leave with finished buckskin. There is no better (or more fun) way to learn this tactile art. Spring and Fall classes. See www.braintan.com/classes for this year's dates. $250.

Recommended Tools and Resources

Ordering information for tools and information that will help you succeed.

Deerskins into Buckskins: The Movie
DVD or VHS • 2 hrs 20 min • $25
By Matt Richards

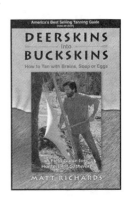

Extremely valuable if you don't have access to hands-on instruction, this video allows you to see each step of this very tactile process. Matt guides you from fresh hide to finished buckskin, taking the time to show you all the textures, motions and details.

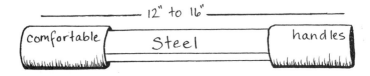

Hide Scrapers $29
made from mill-planer blades

Mill-planer blades make the best scraping tools because they are made of an extremely high quality steel that holds its edge like nothing else. Once properly dulled, you won't need to mess with the edge for the next 100 hides (which probably means your lifetime). These blades come with simple rubber handles.

Softening Cable $8

Everybody's favorite softening tool. These are ¼ inch diameter, five feet long and come with cable clamps. One cable lasts a very long time.

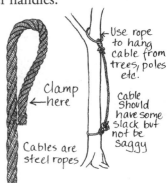

KOH
Wood-ash equivalent

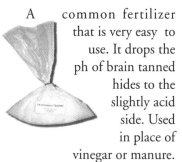

Potassium Hydroxide (KOH) is the active ingredient in wood-ash lye. This man made version is the best substitute for the real thing.

1 lb $4.00
(enough for 8 deer hides)

5 lbs $17.50
(enough for 40 deer hides)

Ammonium Sulphate

A   common fertilizer that is very easy to use. It drops the ph of brain tanned hides to the slightly acid side. Used in place of vinegar or manure.

1 lb $1.95
(enough for 16 deer hides)

5 lbs $9
add $6 extra to shipping.

Pumice $5

Pumice is a volcanic rock that works like natural sandpaper. It'll give your hides a noticeably softer surface texture and speedily remove unwanted membrane and blemishes.

These rocks are hand-selected for us from a volcano in British Columbia. They are nicely rounded and very comfortable to hold and use. One rock will last you at least 50 hides.

Additional copies of this book...

Deerskins into Buckskins $19.95
By Matt Richards

...are available to share with your friends and family who might want to learn to tan their own hides. Hunting friends particularly like learning how to make use of the hides.

braintan.com/buffalo
888 443-3826

Buffalo
Robes
$1195
to
$1895

Buffalo Robes & Rugs

We tan prime, deep winter buffalo hides free of knife cuts. Our hides are worked as soft or softer than any available. Used by tribes and tribal members, movies, museums, and interesting people everywhere.
$1195 = traditional 'robe' size.
$1495 = xl rug, bed spread
$1895 = behemoth
braintan.com/buffalo
Satisfaction Guaranteed!

Wholesale purchases

We offer substantial discounts on bulk purchases of tools, books and videos; to organizations, schools and businesses. For more information write to: customerservice@braintan.com.

Braintan.com

Over 250 pages of articles, tutorials, an ongoing online forum, sources for tools, books, videos, finished skins, and more traditional tanning info than you knew existed.

Shipping	2 ways to order:
Media (videos/books only): $2.75 for first and $1 for each addt'l. **Priority** (tools or tools & media): $7.50 for one tool (except dry-scrapers which are $11.00 to ship) and $2.50 for each addt'l tool (or $4.00 for each addt'l dry-scraper). **International Air**: $14.00 for the first item and $5.00 for each addt'l.	✉ **Mail To:** Traditional Tanner's Supply 1700 East Nevada St Ashland OR 97520 🖱 **Online** at www.braintan.com Checks, M.O's and credit cards **Satisfaction Guaranteed!**